Everyday Indulgences

BIG FLAVORS, BRIGHT COLORS FOR ALL SEASONS

Everyday Indulgences

BIG FLAVORS, BRIGHT COLORS FOR ALL SEASONS

by

JUSTINE DRAKE

Author: Justine Drake
Publisher, Shape SA: Lani Carstens
Photographer: Brandon Amron-Coetzee & Wayne Keet
Text Editor: Kassy Thorne & Nicole Gregory
Director, Mergers & Acquisitions: Jonathan Bigham
VP, International Business Director: Keith Khanlian
International Edition Manager: Angela Kim
EVP, Chief Editorial Director: Bonnie Fuller
Chairman, President, CEO: David Pecker

First published in South Africa in 2004 by Tafelberg Publishers

Contents

how to use this book

This book is divided into the four seasons of the year.
Each season section starts with a description of some
its best flavors (look out for the "Ripe here, right now"
sections), followed by health facts, inspirational ideas.
and lots of delicious recipes.

eat, drink, laugh

Eating and drinking are as much a part of life as breathing and sleeping — and all are immensely pleasurable. But somewhere along the line, guilt — about that extra tummy roll, those burgeoning thighs and the odd hangover — creeps in. Forget all that — work from the premise that deprivation is the source of all bingeing and so, if you go for balance, you're bound to be happier, healthier and slimmer.

I've banned all calorie counting from this book, in part because calorie counts are often misleading, but, more importantly, because the second you start to "count" what you eat, the pleasure is diminished. Also, if you are eating healthy, mostly high-fiber foods and loads of fresh fruit, you naturally eat fewer calories.

Everday Indulgences celebrates balance — of body, mind, soul and thighs. Eat what you crave and own that heady feeling of satiation; minimize that painful hangover by drinking quarts of water and remembering the fun you had; make time for yourself; and sometimes, just sometimes, eat ice cream straight out of the tub.

Know that healthy food isn't steamed, dry, brown or tasteless; but rather fresh, funky and utterly fabulous. Know that the odd bit of exercise will make you feel good and look better, that laughter builds stomach muscles and monks invented champagne, and know that life is for living.

Live all life's flavor.

Justine x.

I'm a sunshine girl — things are brighter and more cheerful, friends reappear, parties abound and the heat adds a new sensuality to just about everything. Tearing yourself out of bed for the early morning run is not as bad when the sun has risen before you, downing the eight-glass daily water quotient is a snap when you really are thirsty, salads are something you

summer

genuinely crave, and summer fruit is so beautiful you're actually driven to eat it. Being healthy and staying in shape is a lot simpler when the sun is out.

tomatoes

OK, so they're on the shelves all year round, but they're at their sweetest, juiciest best in the heat of summer.

tomato truths …

• Tomatoes are rich in the cancer-fighting antioxidant lycopene. Lycopene is more easily absorbed when heated and when served with a little fat — so canned tomatoes and tomato sauce should be added to your shopping list.
• They are relatively high in vitamin C.
• The best bit: they're low in calories, with a large tomato providing only 33 calories.

short order

• Thickly slice fresh tomatoes, drizzle with **extra-virgin olive oil** and a dash of **balsamic vinegar**, and season with sea salt and pepper. Allow to marinate for at least 30 minutes, and serve with crusty bread and fresh basil — the taste of summer.
• Sauté chopped, fresh tomatoes, add a good dollop of **basil pesto**, and stir into pasta — supper in under 10 minutes.
• One of the simplest and most beautiful salads is a mixed tomato salad. Find all the colors, shapes and sizes available, toss together in a large bowl, and marinate in lots of **fresh herbs**, garlic, a dash of sugar, olive oil and vinegar. Transfer to a white platter and serve. It looks as good as it tastes.
• Add a handful of baby tomatoes to your **roasting lamb** 10 minutes before the end of cooking time — they make a bright and juicy addition to the meal.

marinated tomatoes

These will last for up to three weeks in the fridge, and are great squished on bread, or tossed into salads or pastas.

Toss a few packages of baby rosa, cherry and small roma tomatoes onto a baking tray. Add a few unpeeled, bruised garlic cloves, and season with salt and milled pepper. Drizzle with a little olive oil and balsamic vinegar. Roast in a preheated 325°F oven for 15 minutes. Reduce heat to 225°F and bake for a further 2–3 hours. Spoon tomatoes into clean glass jars, sprinkle with sugar and top up with olive oil and a splash of balsamic vinegar. Gently shake to combine flavors and store in the fridge. The tomato-flavored oil is great for salad dressing or pastas.

Pen's penne with tomatoes and feta

My girlfriend Penelope Glover came up with this fab pasta for emergency midweek dinner parties. Do yourself a favor …

1 pound penne
3 C baby rosa tomatoes, whole or halved
4 disks of feta cheese, broken into chunks
2–4 cloves garlic, unpeeled
2 T olive oil
garlic and herb seasoning
a handful of fresh basil or Italian parsley, chopped
Serves 4

Cook pasta according to package instructions. Meanwhile, toss tomatoes, feta, garlic, olive oil and seasoning in an ovenproof dish. Bake in a preheated 350ºF oven for 15–20 minutes. Drain pasta. Toss penne with the feta and tomato mixture, add the herbs and serve immediately.

The tomato mixture can be served — without the pasta — with crusty bread and a green salad for a light lunch.

Good things to add: pitted olives, arugula leaves, balsamic vinegar.

old-fashioned fried tomato sandwich

As a child, this was one of my favorite things to eat — now it's the stuff memories are made of and the best hangover cure I know! *You* decide how decadent you feel: Heat equal amounts of butter and oil in a large frying pan. Arrange about 6 thickly sliced tomatoes in one layer in the pan, and sprinkle with about 1½ t sugar. Season with salt and lots of black pepper. Cook on high for 15–20 minutes, until the tomatoes get squishy and blackened on the edges. While still hot, pile onto fresh white bread, grab a glass of milk and daydream. Serves 4

13

garlic

It's the power-packed clove no self-respecting cook should be without.

go for garlic

• Research is being done into the antimicrobial and antifungal properties of garlic, as well as its potential role in cancer and heart-disease prevention, and even its ability to boost the immune system.

garlic guidelines

• The finer garlic is chopped, the stronger the flavor.
• It is best to slightly brown the onions before adding garlic, as the garlic will brown and burn faster than onion.
• Rub a clove of garlic around the inside of a salad bowl for a sweetly aromatic salad.
• Roast whole garlic, or cut the top of the head off to resemble a flower. Leave the skin on, rub with oil and roast for about an hour in a preheated 350°F oven. Serve with roast meats, or squish the cooked cloves out of their casings and stir into gravies, soups or stews. Or simply spread onto toast with olive oil and sea salt.

bagna cauda

The Italians have a knack for simple, fresh flavors. This dish, which directly translates to "hot bath," is one of them. Don't bother about keeping it hot — it tastes just as good when served at room temperature.

¾ cup + 2 tablespoons extra-virgin olive oil
4 ounces good quality anchovies, chopped
6 garlic cloves, crushed
good pinch of sea salt
Serves 4–6

Place olive oil in a small pot. Toss in anchovies, garlic and sea salt. Cook gently to dissolve the anchovies, but make sure the garlic doesn't brown. Serve warm with chunks of ciabatta and a selection of summer's best raw or steamed vegetables.

moules marinere

These days, we're getting very creative with our mussels — think lemongrass and coriander, or coconut and chili. But who can imagine eating mussels without garlic? I think the traditional French version of mussels, with white wine and garlic, is still the most delicious. Don't even think about using frozen mussels for this dish — buy them fresh or, better, head for the rocks and pick them yourself.

3 T olive oil
2 onions, finely chopped
3 celery stalks with leaves, chopped
about 10 cloves garlic, chopped
1 C dry white wine
2 C chicken, vegetable or fish stock
1 t sugar
sea salt and milled black pepper
4½ pounds fresh mussels
½ C parsley, chopped
Serves 4–6

Discard any open mussels. Heat olive oil in a large saucepan. Add onions, celery and garlic and sauté until glossy, about 5 minutes. Add wine, stock, sugar, sea salt and milled black pepper, and boil for about 5 minutes. Add mussels and parsley. Cover and steam/boil for about 6 minutes. The mussels are ready when the shells have opened. Discard any that don't open.

Spoon into heated bowls and serve with indecent quantities of French bread to mop up the juices.

gremolata

This simple, fresh-flavored topping of finely grated lemon peel, garlic and parsley is traditionally scattered over osso bucco. It's also delicious scattered over roasted vegetables, tossed over boiled new potatoes, sprinkled on roast chicken or in salad dressings. The ratio is equal quantities of finely chopped parsley and finely grated lemon peel to ¼ quantity crushed garlic. You can add an Oriental twist by swapping the parsley for coriander, the lemon peel for lime peel, and adding grated ginger in the same ratio as the garlic.

plums

These plump, purple mouthfuls filled with juicy sweetness look as good as they taste. When they're past their prime, they can be transformed into spicy sauces, tart pickles or sticky jams.

plum potential

• Plums contain flavonoids and are a good source of vitamin A — both of which are antioxidants that mop up potentially harmful free radicals.

plummy pointers

• Choose firm, plump, unwrinkled plums.
• They will keep for up to a week at room temperature, and will continue to ripen if bought when firm.
• The peel is generally tangier than the flesh, and will add a deeper flavor to any dish.
• For a more mellow taste, peel like a tomato by plunging fruit into boiling water for a few minutes, and slipping off the skin.
• Plums freeze well, but unless you want an almond taste to develop, pit the fruit before freezing.
• If making jam, crack the pit to get to the kernel, which enhances flavor.

short order

• **Baked plums** make a quick and **easy dessert**: Drizzle halved plums with fresh orange juice and sprinkle with sugar. Bake in a preheated 350°F oven until soft.
• **Stew plums** slowly in a little **cranberry** or apple juice and eat with low-fat yogurt for **breakfast**.
• Slice ripe plums and toss into a salad with **arugula leaves** and prosciutto ham or goat cheese.
• Whip up a delicious bowl of **plums in red wine**: Make a syrup with 1 C each sugar, red wine and water. Add a dash of **orange liqueur** and a squeeze of lemon juice; bring to a boil, reduce heat and simmer for about 5 minutes. Add about 10 halved, pitted plums and cook gently until soft — about 8–10 minutes. Allow to cool, remove the skins and, if you like, and serve with **frozen yogurt**.

Oriental plum sauce

Sweet 'n sour, hot 'n spicy — this sauce has it all.

1 T olive oil
1 t crushed garlic
1 t freshly grated ginger
1 t dried chili flakes
10 plums, pitted and diced
3 T brown sugar
1 t reduced-sodium soy sauce
1 T medium cream sherry
2 T white wine
1 C water
1 star anise pod
Makes about 2 C

Heat olive oil in a large pot. Add garlic, ginger and chili and sauté for about 2 minutes. Add plums and toss to coat. Add remaining ingredients and cook, covered, for 35–60 minutes, until plums are soft and sauce is reduced and sticky. You can add more water if it evaporates while cooking. Serve blended or chunky, with grilled chicken, or pork or beef fillet.

spiked poached plums

2 C sugar, peel of 1 lemon, juice of ½ lemon, 3 cloves, 5 star anise pods, ½ T black peppercorns. Bring all the ingredients, except plums, to a boil with 1 quart water. Boil for about 10 minutes. Add 4½ pounds washed plums, reduce heat, cover and simmer until plums are soft — about 10–15 minutes. Chill and serve with low-fat yogurt or frozen yogurt, and perhaps a dash of alcohol. Serves 10

go greek

Mediterranean foods are packed with indecent quantities of garlic, lycopene-rich tomatoes and cholesterol-reducing olive oil.

sardines with olives and lemon

Fresh is best, but frozen will do! Sardines are a good source of omega-3 essential fatty acids, which are increasingly being found to have many health benefits, including possibly reducing the risk of heart disease.

12 sardines, cleaned and gutted
1 large red pepper, seeded and cubed
1 red onion, sliced
2 fat cloves garlic, sliced
2 fresh or dried bay leaves
juice of 2 lemons (about ¾ C)
2–3 T olive oil
about 12 Greek kalamata olives, pitted and halved
milled black pepper
2 t Italian parsley, roughly chopped
Serves 4

Arrange sardines, pepper, onion and garlic in a shallow, ovenproof dish. Mix the remaining ingredients together and pour over fish and vegetables. Bake in a preheated 400°F oven for 15–20 minutes. Remove from oven, scatter with parsley and serve with crusty bread or rice, and a green salad.

keftedes

These meatballs in tomato are usually fried before they are baked — but why add the extra calories when you can simply simmer them in tomato sauce?

meatballs

½ pound ground beef
½ pound ground pork or veal
3 slices white bread, crusts removed
1 onion, very finely chopped
3 cloves garlic, crushed
4 t dried oregano
sea salt and milled black pepper

Mix all ingredients together thoroughly. Pat into oval-shaped balls and set aside.

tomato sauce

1 T olive oil
1 onion, finely chopped
3 cloves garlic, crushed
10 large, ripe tomatoes, peeled and chopped
14-ounce can tomato purée (not paste)
1 t sugar
sea salt and milled black pepper
fresh oregano
Serves 6

Heat oil and add onion and garlic. Sauté for 3 minutes. Add remaining ingredients and bring to a boil. Reduce heat, cover and simmer for 15–30 minutes. Arrange meatballs in an ovenproof dish. Pour over sauce and bake in a preheated 350°F oven for 30 minutes, uncovered. Scatter with lots of fresh oregano and serve with orzo (small rice-shaped noodles, also known as risoni) and a green salad or steamed green beans.

souvlaki

You can use beef, fish, chicken, pork or lamb for these kebabs — it's the basting sauce that gives it the Greek flavor. I add a few ingredients to the kebab because every old classic could do with a new twist now and then.

basting sauce

¼ C olive oil
2 T freshly squeezed lemon juice
1 T dried oregano
2 cloves garlic
crushed sea salt and milled black pepper
Makes enough for 6–8 kebabs

kebabs

1 pound pork fillet or fresh tuna, cubed
fresh bay leaves — optional
3 lemons, cut into chunks
Serves 4

Mix all the basting ingredients together. Thread the meat or fish, bay leaves and/or lemons onto wooden or metal skewers. If you're using wooden skewers, soak them in water for about 30 minutes to prevent them from burning during grilling. Brush kebabs with basting sauce. Cook over hot coals or under a preheated grill, basting frequently, until done. Serve with hot pita bread, garlicky tzatziki, and a peasant salad of chopped tomatoes, cucumber and onion, tossed with dried oregano, salt, milled pepper, lemon juice and olive oil.

eggplant and feta bake

Serve as a vegetable side dish, or as a main course with crusty bread and a green salad.

2 large eggplants, sliced lengthways
1 T olive oil
1 large onion, finely chopped
3 cloves garlic, crushed
2 red peppers, seeded and chopped
8 ripe tomatoes, peeled* and chopped
1 t sugar
sea salt and milled black pepper
2 T mixed fresh herbs — oregano,
   Italian parsley and basil
4½ ounces feta cheese
Serves 4

Lightly brush sliced eggplant with olive oil. Grill until golden under a preheated grill, or in a griddle pan. Meanwhile, make a fat-free tomato and pepper sauce: Place onion, garlic, peppers, tomatoes, sugar, seasoning and herbs in a pot. Cover and bring to the boil. Reduce heat, remove lid and simmer for 20–30 minutes, until the sauce is thick and still quite chunky. Lightly spray an oven-to-table dish with olive oil spray. Begin with a layer of grilled eggplant. Spoon over a layer of tomato sauce, and crumble over about 3 T feta. Repeat until all ingredients are used, ending with a layer of eggplant. Bake in a preheated 400°F oven for 20 minutes. Serve with crusty bread and a green salad.
*To peel tomatoes, make a shallow cross in the bottom of each tomato, plunge into boiling water and leave for 5–10 minutes. Remove and the skins will slip off.

grilled calamari

Wash calamari and pat dry. Spray a heavy-based grill pan with olive oil spray and heat until smoking hot. Cook tentacles, one at a time, until they turn white and curl slightly, about 3–5 minutes. Remove from pan, season and drizzle with fresh lemon juice and olive oil. Serve with wedges of lime. These also work very well on the barbecue.

things on sticks

It's terribly difficult to look elegant laden with a handbag, glass of wine and a plate of food. So, to ensure you and your friends look good at all times, I've come up with the ultimate cocktail party solution — stick food!

Italian summer on a stick

Prosciutto ham and melon — it doesn't get much better than this.
You'll need cantaloupe, winter melon or honeydew melon, peeled and cut into thick sticks, prosciutto ham, thinly sliced, olive oil, milled pepper. Wrap melon in a liberal layer of prosciutto. Drizzle each stick with a little fruity olive oil and season with milled pepper. Serve immediately.

stick sense

• Use things on sticks for cocktail parties, or as a pre-dinner or pre-barbecue snack.
• Barbecue sausage before you start the rest of the food for the barbecue. Serve on sticks with sweet chili sauce, Thai-style plum sauce (see p. 20) or your favorite chutney.

use

• Bamboo sticks: You can get medium-thin bamboo sticks from Asian stores.
• Wooden skewers: If you are going to cook the threaded ingredients, soak the sticks in water for about 30 minutes before use to prevent them from burning.
• Metal skewers
• Rosemary stalks: Remove the leaves from the bottom of the stalk and wash well before threading.
• Lemongrass: Remove the outer leaves and use the whole stalk as a stick.
• Toothpicks for smaller items.
• Dried river reeds if you can get your hands on them.

quick sticks

• Marinate **tofu cubes** in minced ginger and soy sauce for about 30 minutes. Thread onto skewers with rehydrated **seaweed** or wilted spinach. Dip tofu into toasted **sesame seeds** for added crunch.
• Marinate baby **mozzarella balls** (boccocini) in pesto and a little olive oil. Thread onto sticks with strips of **roasted peppers** or halved cherry tomatoes, marinated in garlic, balsamic vinegar and **olive oil**.
• Marinate peeled **shrimp** (with their tails) in lemon juice, salt and milled pepper. Spear two or three shrimp onto the top end of a skewer and serve with a **spicy fruit salsa**. Make the salsa using ripe papaya, finely chopped red chili, **coriander**, fresh lemon or orange juice and a little sugar.

tandoori chicken and mango

These colors look great threaded onto fake porcupine quills.

8 chicken fillets, cut in half, and lengthways into strips
olive oil
2 T tandoori paste
1 T chutney
1 C plain yogurt
juice of 1 lemon
2 mangoes, peeled and cut into long slivers*
handful of coriander
salt and ground pepper
Serves 10

Combine yogurt, paste, chutney and lemon juice. Pour over chicken. Refrigerate and marinate for at least two hours, or preferably overnight. Place chicken on a baking tray, brush with marinade and grill for 10 minutes, basting occasionally to keep them moist. Allow chicken to cool slightly. Thread chicken onto fake porcupine quills and lay mango on top. Serve at room temperature.

Note: If this is too much for the brain, buy ready-made chicken tikka (kekab) strips.

*If mangoes are out of season, canned ones also work.

tuna and cucumber rolls

The lemon juice "cooks" the tuna

1 pound sashimi-quality tuna, cut into large
  chunks
1 T garlic, crushed
1 T minced ginger
juice of 1 big lemon
juice of 1 orange
1 t brown sugar
1 T fish sauce
1 cucumber

dipping sauce
2 red chilies
½ C white wine vinegar
5 T white sugar
2 T fresh lime juice
1 T fish sauce
Serves 10

Place tuna chunks into a shallow dish. Mix garlic, ginger, citrus juices, sugar and fish sauce together and pour over tuna. Allow to marinate for about two hours. Meanwhile, blend dipping sauce ingredients together and set aside. Using a potato peeler, shave long ribbons of cucumber and cut in half. Drain tuna. Wrap a piece of tuna with the cucumber ribbon and secure with a lemongrass stick, simple bamboo skewer or whatever else you like. Serve with the dipping sauce on the side.

beets and creamy feta

Marinated creamy Danish-style feta cheese (look for it in delis and good supermarkets) with crisp slices of raw beet. Unexpected and sublime.

about 11 ounces Danish-style feta cheese
½ C extra-virgin olive oil
handful fresh oregano, broken into leaves
2 cloves garlic, sliced
4 large beets
Serves 10

Cut feta into bite-sized cubes, and place in a shallow dish. Mix oil, herbs and garlic and pour over. Marinate at room temperature for at least an hour, and preferably overnight. Place beets in cold water and bring to a boil. Remove from heat and allow to cool in water. Peel off outer skin (it is easier to do this after blanching than before). Using a swivel-head potato peeler, peel around the circumference of the beets to create ribbons. Thread onto skewers and top with feta and a sprig of fresh oregano.
Note: Cut calories and use reduced-fat feta instead — not as delicious, but at least it will save the hips!

cool food

Take the heat out of entertaining by serving chilled snacks. Or add an ingredient or two, change the serving dish and transform your snack into a main meal.

glass noodles with chili and sautéed garlic

To create a main course salad, add strips of grilled chicken breasts or pan-fried shrimp, and serve the noodles in bowls instead of glasses.

8 whole garlic cloves, thinly sliced
olive oil spray
¼ pound rice vermicelli
3 fresh red chilies, seeded and sliced into thin strips
4 green onions, sliced very thinly on the slant
½ packet (½ ounce) coriander, chopped

dressing:

½ T sesame oil
1 T rice wine vinegar
2 T fresh lemon or lime juice
1 t sugar or palm sugar
1 t freshly grated ginger
1 C water
½ T light soy sauce
sea salt and milled black pepper to taste
1 T pickled ginger, chopped very finely (optional)
Serves 8–10

Spray a non-stick pan with olive oil spray and heat. Reduce heat to low and sauté garlic until pale gold and slightly soft — 3–5 minutes. You will need to keep an eye on it, as it burns easily. Set aside. Cook noodles according to instructions, drain and cool. Toss noodles with garlic, chili, green onion and coriander. Mix dressing ingredients together and pour over noodles. Pile into small glasses or bowls and serve with chopsticks or cocktail forks.
Note: The pan-fried garlic is very pungent, so don't add too far in advance, otherwise all you'll taste is garlic!

Moroccan lettuce wraps

If you'd prefer to serve this as a lunch or dinner option, simply serve each ingredient in a separate bowl. Add hot basmati rice, and guests can make up their own lettuce wraps. You may also want to add a few extra ingredients — grated carrot, celery strips, shredded chili, chives, etc.

4 chicken breasts, skinless and boneless
1 t olive oil
3 T chermoulah paste
2 butter lettuces
4–6 green onions
about ¼ C fat-free yogurt
about half a cucumber, cut into thin matchsticks
2 beets, peeled and finely shredded
juice of 2 limes
sea salt and milled black pepper
Serves 8–12

Cut chicken into strips. Toss strips in chermoulah paste to coat. If time allows, marinate for 1–3 hours. Heat olive oil in a non-stick pan and stir-fry chicken for about 5 minutes or until done. Set aside to cool. Spread a little yogurt on each lettuce leaf, add chicken, green onions, cucumber and beets. Drizzle with lime juice and season. Roll up and secure with string or a toothpick.

chilled smoked salmon and potato soup

Simply change the serving vessel to suit the occasion.

½ C water
1 t olive oil
1 large onion, finely chopped
3 potatoes, peeled and diced
4 C chicken stock
1½ C fat-free milk
juice of 1 lime
½ pound smoked salmon
milled black pepper
Serves 4–6

Heat olive oil and water in a large pot. Reduce heat to low and sauté onions for 3 minutes, until soft and glassy – they must not be brown. Add potatoes and toss to coat. Cook for 2 minutes and add stock and milk. Simmer on low heat for about 20 minutes or until potatoes are cooked. Cool slightly before transferring to a blender. Add lime juice and salmon and blend until smooth. Season and chill until needed. Serve topped with salmon roe, lumpfish or caviar, or simply sprinkle with herbs.
Note: Cut costs by using smoked salmon off-cuts instead of slices.

boiled eggs
with parsley drizzle

To create a light lunch dish, serve these eggs on a bed of salad leaves with thinly sliced red onion and chunks of canned tuna in water.

Place 6 free-range eggs in boiling water and cook for 3 minutes. Remove from heat, cover with a tight-fitting lid and allow to stand for a further 3 minutes. Rinse eggs under cold water and peel gently. Blend or pound together 1 T Italian parsley leaves, 1 T chives, 1 t white balsamic vinegar and 1 T olive oil. Season well and drizzle over halved eggs just before serving. Serves 12 as a snack and 4–6 as a salad

Summer's heat recedes into plain sunshine, and a new chill fills the night air. A russet-colored carpet of leaves hides the earth, and there are few weekends left for country picnics and mountain river dips. Night falls earlier, dinners become longer, and lazy Sunday breakfasts make a

autumn

comeback. Autumn is here, and with it indecently erotic figs, deep purple beets and the sweetest orange carrots. Grocers' shelves are packed with the new season's juicy citrus and life — well, it just got cozier.

beets

Grandmother's staple has gone mainstream, and it's no wonder — the color is almost as alluring as the taste.

beet bonus

• Beets are a source of fiber that has been shown to reduce the risk of some types of cancer.

• Beets make a great juice if you have a juice extractor, but don't get a shock if your urine turns pink.

beets bits

• Don't peel beets before boiling — it's a laborious job when they're raw, but once they're boiled the skin literally falls away.

• To ensure even cooking, choose vegetables of the same size, and with skins intact. Do not scrub. Cut off leaves about 2 inches above root and wash well. Boil, roast or microwave.

• Medium-sized beets will cook in lightly salted water in 30–45 minutes.

• Baby beets are the sweetest. You can eat the whole beets and they're great to roast.

• The sweetness of beets is best balanced by either acid (citrus juices or balsamic vinegar) or creamy flavors like yogurt, feta cheese, goat cheese, or creamed horseradish. Other good flavor partners include ginger, chili pepper, mint, basil and dill.

short order

• Boil, peel, slice and drizzle with balsamic vinegar, olive oil and seasoning. Allow to **marinate** for at least an hour. Just before serving, toss with chopped **mint** or basil and serve. Good additions are fresh segments of orange or crumbled reduced-fat feta cheese.

• Add chopped beets to a **salsa** with chopped red onions, tomatoes and herbs like coriander and Italian parsley, and dress with balsamic vinegar, orange juice, a dash of **chili pepper**, olive oil, and sea salt and milled black pepper.

• Use a potato peeler to peel thin slices of **raw beets** and add to your favorite salad.

• **Go Russian** and make borscht (hot or cold beet soup). Cook beets, onions, potatoes, carrots and garlic together. Purée and flavor with lemon juice, **dill** or parsley, and yogurt. Serve with boiled new potatoes.

• Whip up a **great dip** with puréed beets and **chickpeas**, flavor and thin with tahini, lemon juice, garlic and yogurt, and season well. Serve with raw vegetables or crusty bread.

an up-beet tart

A bit extravagant on the calorie front, but worth well it!

1 x 14-ounce roll puff pastry*
6 medium beets
1 T olive oil
1 t dried chili pepper
3 T balsamic vinegar
1 T sugar
4 disks goat cheese
1½ C ricotta
1 bunch of chives, chopped
7 T fat-free yogurt
sea salt and milled black pepper
handful Italian parsley, chopped
Serves 6

Pastry: Preheat oven to 400°F. Roll pastry into a rectangular shape and place on a lightly oiled baking tray. Cut ½-inch strips of pastry, brush with milk and press along the edges to form a sort of box. Bake for 15–20 minutes.

Beets: Boil beets until cooked through. Cool, peel and cut into wedges. Heat olive oil in a pan and add chili pepper, balsamic vinegar and sugar. Fry for 1 minute. Add beets and sauté over a medium-high heat to glaze. Mash together goat cheese, ricotta, yogurt, chives and salt and pepper. Remove pastry case from oven and allow to cool. Fill with cheese mixture and top with beets. Serve topped with chopped Italian parsley.

*To cut calories, substitute with 4 sheets phyllo dough, spritzed with olive oil spray between layers. Watch your cooking times.

red risotto

Cook, skin and chop 6 small beets. Purée half and set aside. In a large pot, heat 1½ quarts chicken or vegetable stock and the juice of 1 orange. Heat 1 T olive oil in a large, deep frying pan, add 1 fat clove crushed garlic, 1 chopped red pepper and 1 finely chopped onion. Gently sauté for 3 minutes. Add beets purée and cook for 3 minutes. Add 12 ounces Arborio rice and cook for 5 minutes, stirring frequently. Add 4 large, ripe chopped tomatoes and the finely sliced peel of 1 orange and a ladle of hot stock. Cook slowly, stirring until the liquid is absorbed. Continue stirring and adding stock until the rice has swollen and is just cooked — about 15–20 minutes. Add the remaining beets and adjust seasoning. Remove from heat, drizzle with olive oil, add chives and serve.
Serves 4 as a main course or 6 as a side dish

carrots

A million bunnies can't be wrong.

carrot goodness

- Carrots are one of the best sources of beta carotene, the antioxidant that's converted to vitamin A in the body. It fights free radicals, and helps prevent cell damage and certain cancers.
- There are about 24 calories in a medium-sized carrot.

short order

- For health, energy and the feel-good factor, there's no better way to start the day than with an ice-cold **carrot and fruit juice drink** — you'll need a juicer for this. Juice a few fresh carrots (about 1 pound will give you a glass), a small knob of **fresh ginger**, and add orange, apple or ruby grapefruit juice to taste.
- There's no better accompaniment to a **Sunday roast** than carrots, parsnips and potatoes mashed together with butter (although olive oil will do), chopped parsley and lots of salt and pepper. Mix things up with **sweet potato** and carrot, especially if you're serving game.
- Low-fat **carrot chips** are great for cocktail parties. Slice lengthways as thinly as possible. Spray a baking tray with cooking spray, and bake in a preheated 250ºF oven for 1–2 hours, until crisp. Lightly sprinkle with **sea salt** and serve hot or cold.
- Carrots and dill work wonderfully together as a **side dish** that's particularly good with fish. Using a potato peeler, peel carrots into thin ribbons and steam or stir-fry until cooked. Toss with sea salt, olive oil and **fresh dill**.
- Make a batch of low-fat **caramelized carrots**: Cook carrots, with a few cloves of garlic and a dash of sugar, in a small amount of stock. When the carrots are done and the stock has almost cooked away, add a dash of lemon juice and **balsamic vinegar**. Cook to brown and caramelize, and season to taste.
- Steam or boil whole baby carrots and toss with **toasted cumin** or caraway seeds, sea salt and olive oil.

carrots baked in foil

You can make one large parcel or 4 individual ones.

1 pound young carrots, preferably with their tops
3 T olive oil
2 T freshly squeezed orange juice
1 T caraway or cumin seeds, toasted
sea salt and milled black pepper
Serves 4

Preheat oven to 425°F. Peel or scrub carrots. Lay out a double piece of foil or baking paper. Fold up the sides and place carrots in the center. Mix together the olive oil, orange juice and caraway or cumin seeds in a small container, and pour over carrots. If necessary, divide liquid equally between individual parcels. Toss well, close parcels and bake for about 45 minutes.

Moroccan carrot salad

Toasted cumin seeds make a world of difference to flavor, and it only takes a few minutes to do.

Boil 2¼ pounds peeled carrots and 1 clove garlic in salted water until just tender (not soft). Drain and reserve the garlic. Thinly slice carrots or peel into ribbons. If you have a mortar and pestle, now is the time to use it; if not, simply mix the ingredients with a certain amount of force. Pound the boiled garlic, ½ t toasted cumin seeds and a pinch of salt together. Add the juice of ½ a large lemon, ½ t superfine sugar and 1 T olive oil, and mix well. Toss the carrots with the cumin mixture and add a handful of fresh coriander. Serve at room temperature. Serves 2–4

figs

Soft, squishy and utterly delicious,
figs truly are a gift from the gods.

fig health

- Dried figs are higher in carbohydrates and calories than their fresh counterparts.
- Dried figs contain relatively high amounts of fiber.

short order

- Wrap slices of salty **prosciutto ham** around luscious sweet figs, drizzle with olive oil and eat with hot, crusty bread.
- Poach whole figs in **white wine**, sugar and cinnamon until plump and squishy but still holding their shape. Serve with a dollop of low-fat yogurt.
- Simmer 1 cup **port** until it is syrupy — about 5 minutes. Place 4 quartered figs in a shallow dish and pour over syrup. Leave to stand for 5 minutes and serve as a pudding, or spread on lightly toasted fruit bread with **ricotta cheese** for brunch.
- Slit 4 figs from the top almost to the bottom. Drizzle with **honey** and grill for 5 minutes. Toss into a salad of watercress, arugula, basil and **bocconcini** (baby mozzarella balls); dress with a honey/lemon vinaigrette.
- Whip up a **chicken liver** and lean bacon salad. Trim and halve ⅔ pound chicken livers; pat dry and dust with flour. Cook in olive oil for 4–5 minutes until brown but still pink inside. Grill **lean bacon** until crisp; cool and crumble into a bowl. Toss quartered figs, arugula, baby spinach leaves and bacon bits with olive oil and lemon juice. Add hot chicken livers, season, toss and serve immediately.
- **Preserve figs** in red wine while they are still in season. Place 1½ pounds superfine sugar, 1 cup red wine, 2 T red wine vinegar, ½ t whole cloves, 1 **stick cinnamon** and a 1-inch piece of peeled, sliced ginger in a heavy-based saucepan and slowly bring to a boil. Reduce heat and simmer until sugar has dissolved. Trim fig stems and prick several times with a small knife. Place figs in a saucepan and simmer gently until **syrup** is very thick and the figs are dark and almost translucent — about 2 hours. Spoon into hot, sterilized jars, and seal. Enjoy with **runny cheeses** and warm baguettes.

fig and nut roll

If you need a sweet fix, enlist dried figs to make this really quick fig, date and nut log to serve with coffee or crackers and cheese. If you can't find fresh dates, replace their weight with an additional weight of figs.

7 ounces soft dried figs, finely chopped
7 ounces fresh dates, pitted and chopped
2 T red or white Muscatel or Marsala wine
1 T freshly grated ginger, optional
4 T pistachios
Serves 10

Set aside half of the chopped figs. Process remaining figs, dates, Muscatel or Marsala and ginger in a food processor until mixture is coarsely puréed and forms a soft ball. Transfer to a clean work surface and knead in reserved chopped figs and pistachios. Shape into a roll, about 2 x 7 inches. Wrap log loosely in foil and stand in a cool, dry place for 3–4 days to dry slightly, then wrap in foil and refrigerate. This fig "salami" will keep in the fridge for up to 2 months.

fig and goat cheese pizza

Make this deliciously different pizza to serve with snacks or as a light lunch.

Brush plain, good-quality pizza crusts or foccacia with olive oil, season well with salt and pepper, and bake according to instructions, for half the suggested time.

Top half-baked pizza with wedges of fresh fig, crumbled goat cheese, torn pieces of smoked beef and sprigs of fresh thyme. Drizzle with olive oil and bake in a preheated 400°F oven until pizza is golden and figs and cheese have begun to melt.

Serve with a crisp, green salad.

Serves 4

the big breakfast

Cereal is for Monday to Friday, and boiled eggs are great family fare, but weekend brunches with friends call for innovation and celebration.

steamed asparagus with salmon roe

vegetables

• **Fresh:** Organize platters of thickly sliced, ripe tomatoes, sprinkled with salt and pepper, drizzled with olive oil and topped with **fresh basil**; sliced cucumber with **peppery olive oil** and sea salt; large bowls of crisp, fresh **arugula leaves**. Cool steamed asparagus and serve straight or wrapped with paper-thin slices of **prosciutto ham** or smoked salmon. **Avocado** is always yummy, sliced and simply dressed with fresh lemon juice, sea salt and milled black pepper.

• **Cooked:** Try large black **mushrooms** roasted at 350°F for 15 minutes in olive oil and water, topped with sautéed garlic. Roast halved **cherry tomatoes** for 10 minutes at 350°F and serve with baby mushrooms and fresh herbs. Thickly slice tomato, sprinkle with a little sugar and lots of black pepper, and grill. Hot spears of grilled or steamed **asparagus** are divine with eggs, as are thickly sliced, boiled potatoes, served warm with herbs, drizzled with olive oil. **Wilted spinach** leaves (steamed or stir-fried) are great with creamy egg dishes — if you add some garlic and bit of fresh **chili pepper**, so much the better. **Stir-fried peppers** (yellow, red and orange) look as good as they taste as part of a brunch table — toss in a handful of **fresh herbs** and serve them in the pan.

fruit

In summer, **simple platters** or bowls of fresh fruit are divine. Peel and slice the fruit, drizzle with a little **fresh orange juice** and perhaps add a dollop of **passion fruit pulp**. Fresh mint and lemon verbena work well as a garnish or as a flavor enhancer for fresh fruit.

• When **soft summer fruit** (plums, apricots, peaches, nectarines) starts to get a little dodgy around the edges, instead of tossing it, poach it. Use fruit juice, water, **sparkling wine** or a combination of these to make up the cooking liquid, sweeten with sugar or honey, and flavor with things like **vanilla beans**, cinnamon sticks or **star anise**. Winter fruit compotes made with fresh and **dried fruits** can be equally delicious. Just remember, though, that dried fruit is naturally sweet, so leave out the sugar and cook the fruit in a mixture of fruit juice and water.

mini potato and
rosemary frittatas

eggs

• Whip up mini **baked frittatas**. Parboil 1 pound new potatoes — they should be cooked but still firm. Preheat the oven to 350ºF. Line 4–6 individual tart pans with foil, and spray with olive oil spray. Slice potatoes, arrange in the pans, and sprinkle with **rosemary**. Lightly beat 4 eggs with a little milk, pour over potatoes and bake for 6–8 minutes. Finish under the grill for a puffy golden look. Frittatas can also be done in a pan. Fry goodies (see below) in a little olive oil or **bubbling chicken stock**, add the beaten eggs and cook slowly, to avoid burning, until almost set. Place under a preheated grill to brown and set the middle.

Try these **combos**: potato, onion and rosemary (very **Spanish**); mixed peppers and goat cheese; avocado and **green onion** (fry the onion only; add the avocado when you add the egg); fresh **asparagus** and cherry tomato (brilliant finished with a sprinkling of feta).

• Large platters of thick 'n creamy **scrambled eggs** always go down well. The secret lies in very slow cooking and constant stirring — that way you won't need to add loads of cream and butter like they do for hotel buffets. Serve sprinkled with fresh herbs or with bits of **smoked salmon**, tossed in only once the pot has been removed from the heat. Remember that the eggs will continue to cook once removed from the heat, so stop cooking a minute or two before they look ready.

• Ultra-trendy and totally divine are **egg rolls** (very thin egg pancakes). Whip up a couple of eggs, season and toss with herbs. Pour a small amount of the mixture (about 2 T) into a small non-stick pan, and cook for about 45 seconds; flip, and cook on the other side. Repeat until you have a large stack — you'll need them. Serve as is, or roll with **smoked salmon**, prosciutto ham or low-fat cream cheese with asparagus spears and **squishy tomatoes** on the side.

baked ricotta with
roasted vine tomatoes

cheese

• **Baked ricotta** is a totally fabulous brunch dish, served with savory things like squishy tomatoes or stir-fried peppers, and crisp, low-fat grilled **chipped beef**. You could also serve it with a fruit compote (in which case, leave out the salt, pepper and herbs and add spices like **cinnamon** and **nutmeg**). Mix 3 C ricotta cheese with 3 lightly whisked egg whites. Stir in a handful of fresh herbs and season to taste. Spray a deep oven-proof dish or cake tin with olive oil cooking spray and spoon in mixture. Drizzle with olive oil and bake in a preheated 350°F oven for 20 minutes. Allow to cool slightly and invert onto a warmed serving dish.

• Other cheese options include fat-free Philadelphia cream cheese, low-fat smooth or chunky **cottage cheese**, fresh ricotta, hard and soft goat cheese and **reduced-fat Cheddar**.

bakes

Buttery croissants and Danishes are all very well, but if you're thinking healthy, rather opt for:

• **Bran muffins** — best if you make them yourself, otherwise they can be laced with hidden fats.

• Nutty whole-wheat, sourdough and **crusty Italian** are good bread choices.

• Raisin or **cinnamon loaf** is great toasted and served with baked ricotta and a fruit compote.

breakfast stack — grilled black mushrooms with a tumble of sautéed baby mushrooms, cherry tomatoes and fresh basil, topped with grilled chipped beef

meat and fish

• Opt for lean turkey bacon, and if you must have sausages, go for **low-fat porkers**, or turkey sausages.

• Experiment with chicken and turkey **bacon** — they usually need less cooking time due to their **reduced fat** content.

• Chipped **beef** is divine grilled, and relatively low in fat. The beef cooks very fast: Pop under a preheated grill for a minute or two and remove, and the meat will crisp once cool.

• Smoked **salmon** and trout go down well, and with a glass of **champagne**, transform brunch into a feast.

• Mackerel, haddock and **kippered herring** are wonderfully healthy options.

• **Oysters** are the last word in posh brunch nibbles, and they're also great tossed into a **Bloody Mary** — but then your guests might still be there at dinnertime.

drinks

• **Sparkling wine** or champagne, with or without fruit juice, and Bloody Marys are the most common.

• **Gin and tonic** is perfectly acceptable at the brunch hour.

• **Smoothies** are great but rather filling, unless you use only fruit — use **frozen** chunks of assorted fresh fruit, thinned with a little fruit juice, for the slushiest creations.

• Fresh fruit juices, carafes of water filled with sliced lemon and mint, and **iced tea** are all great.

• Make "**caffe freddo**" (iced coffee) — brew strong espresso, leave to chill, and serve very cold, with crushed ice in shot glasses, or in a tall glass with **low-fat ice cream**. Or, mix coffee with hot skim milk and brown sugar to taste. Leave to chill and serve poured over **ice cubes**.

frozen berries blended with fresh orange juice

spice sense

Cut back on fat and bulk up on flavor
with spice mixes, rubs and pastes.

spice sense

• Spices come from various plant parts: **seeds** (cumin, coriander, cardamom, mustard), **berries** (peppercorns, allspice), **buds** (cloves), **bark** (cinnamon) and **leaves** (curry leaves and dried lime leaves). Choose **whole spices** over ground: they keep their pungency much longer and can be easily ground. Fresh ginger, garlic and **lemongrass** are essential to certain dishes, where the dried variety just wouldn't do.

• **Dry-roasting** enhances the flavors of most spices and makes them easier to crush. Heat a small pan to very hot, add spices and cook for 2–3 minutes until spices are dark brown and the smell fills the kitchen. Shake the pan often to prevent burning. Remove and grind using a mortar and pestle, or in a coffee grinder.

• **Crushing** or grinding releases the flavors of spices, but the harder ones (cinnamon, turmeric, dried ginger) are a problem to crush at home, so buy these in powdered form. **Grind spice** as you need it and not more than two days in advance. Harder seeds like coriander, **fenugreek** and allspice are easily ground in a pepper mill. Small seeds like cumin, fennel, **caraway** and cloves can be ground using a mortar and pestle. Grind in a circular motion. This is also a good technique for fresh ingredients like herbs, garlic, ginger and larger chilies.

• Sometimes, **infusion** (when you release the flavor in liquid) is the way to go. **Saffron** is often infused in water or milk. Ginger can be infused by placing large chunks into the cooking liquid — the result is a more mellow, less intense flavor.

• **Bruising** or crushing is the magic technique with spices like lemongrass, cardamom, **juniper** and ginger.

cajun chicken with coriander, corn and tomato salsa

Cajun spice mix

Prepare the dry spices first and refrigerate. Add onion and garlic only when you are ready to use.

1 t peppercorns
1 t cumin seeds
1 t white mustard seeds
2 t paprika
1 t cayenne pepper
1 t dried oregano
2 t dried thyme
1 t sea salt
2 garlic cloves
1 onion, chopped
Makes about ½ C

Dry-roast the peppercorns, cumin and white mustard seeds to release flavors. Grind to a fine powder and add paprika, cayenne, oregano, thyme and salt, and grind again. When ready to use, add garlic and onion to spices and blend to form a chunky paste.

short order

• Score **chicken breast** fillets and rub with the spice mixture. Grill or pan-fry until done. Serve with a coriander, corn and tomato salsa.
• Add lemon juice and olive oil to the Cajun spice mix. Rub over oily fish like yellowtail, **tuna** or salmon. Bake in a hot oven or barbecue over the coals. Serve with a fresh coriander and **cucumber relish** (mix grated cucumber with fresh chopped coriander). Season with sea salt and a little lemon juice.
• Toss **potato wedges** in the spice mixture. Drizzle with a little olive oil and bake in a 400°F oven until done, about 30 minutes. Serve as a snack with drinks or as an accompaniment to roast chicken.
• Add a little oil to the spice mix and rub over halved **pita bread**. Toast and top with avocado, red onion, fresh basil and lemon juice.

Thai green curry paste

10 fresh green chilies

½ onion, sliced

4 garlic cloves

1 stalk lemongrass, lower part of stem bruised and sliced

4 sprigs coriander, stems and leaves

4 t peanut oil

1 t grated lemon peel

1 t shrimp paste, dry cooked for 2–3 minutes

1 T coriander seeds

2 t cumin seeds

1 t salt

Makes about ½ cup

Pound the first six ingredients using a mortar and pestle or blend in a food processor, gradually adding the oil. Add the lemon peel and shrimp paste. Dry-roast cumin and coriander seeds, grind to a powder, and add to the paste. Use immediately or keep for 3–4 weeks in the fridge.

short order

• Whip up a simple **Thai curry** by stir-frying 2 T of the Thai green curry paste in 1 T oil until aromatic. Add 1 pound cubed butternut, 1 can reduced-fat coconut milk, 1 C chicken or vegetable stock, 2 T fish sauce, 1 T brown sugar and the juice of ½ lime. Cook until tender. Just before serving, toss in a handful of peeled, cooked shrimp and some fresh coriander.

• Heat the curry paste in a pot until aromatic. Add cooked **noodles**, baby tomatoes and chicken stock. Heat through and serve.

• Rub the paste under the skin of a **whole chicken** and roast as usual. Serve with jasmine rice and a bowl of plain yogurt with chopped mint.

• Stir-fry **strips of pork** or chicken and red peppers in the curry paste. Toss in cooked rice and fresh herbs, and heat through.

green curry with shrimp and coconut

basic Indian curry powder

8 dried red chilies

8 T coriander seeds

4 T cumin seeds

2 fenugreek seeds

2 t black mustard seeds

2 t black peppercorns

2 t garam masala

1 T ground turmeric

1 t ground ginger

6–8 curry leaves

Makes about 1 cup

Remove stalks and seeds from chilies. Dry-fry with the next six ingredients, shaking pan, so as not to burn spices, and to release the rich aroma. Grind to a powder using a mortar and pestle or in a coffee grinder, then stir in turmeric, ginger and curry leaves.

short order

• Fry 1 chopped onion and a few cloves of crushed garlic in 1 T oil. Add 2 T curry powder and cook to release aroma. Add 2 cans of drained **chickpeas**, 2 chopped tomatoes and 2 C vegetable stock. Cook for 10 minutes. Add a handful of spinach and allow to wilt. Serve with mint yogurt and naan bread.

• Whip up a simple mixed **potato curry**. Fry 1 large onion and 4 cloves garlic in a little oil. Add curry powder and cook to release aroma. Add a mixture of 4 chopped sweet potatoes and 2 regular potatoes, and about 4 cups chicken stock. Season. Cook until potatoes are tender. Purée and serve with **caramelized onions** and a dollop of yogurt.

• Toss **root vegetables** in the curry powder and a bit of oil. Roast until done and serve with wedges of fresh lime or lemon.

• A new take on **mussels:** Fry onion and curry powder in a bit of oil. Add stock, white wine, reduced-fat coconut milk and loads of fresh coriander. Bring to a boil, add mussels, cover and cook until mussels open. Serve with basmati rice.

juicy fruit

The bright, happy colors of citrus lend a
cheerful contrast to the earthy shades of
autumn, and their tart, fresh flavors add zing
to even the most basic meal.

roasted pumpkin, tomato and orange soup

Roasting pumpkin enhances its sweet flavor, and the acidity of orange and tomato balance this satisfying autumn soup.

about 3–4 C peeled pumpkin chunks
1 T brown sugar
4 T olive oil
1 large onion, peeled and chopped
2 cloves garlic, crushed
1 t freshly minced ginger
1 t crushed, dried chili
2 celery stalks (with leaves), chopped
juice and finely grated peel of 1 orange
2 x 14-ounce cans peeled tomatoes
3 C vegetable or chicken stock
sea salt and milled black pepper
Serves 4–6

Place pumpkin chunks in a roasting pan and toss to coat with brown sugar and 2 T olive oil. Roast in a preheated 350°F oven until soft — about 20–30 minutes.

Meanwhile, heat remaining olive oil in a large pot. Add onion, garlic, ginger and chili, and sauté for about 3 minutes. Add celery and sauté for 2–3 minutes. Add orange juice and grated peel, tomatoes (with juice) and stock. Add roasted pumpkin and any pan juices and bring to the boil. Reduce heat and simmer for 20 minutes. Season to taste. Purée if you want a smooth soup. Serve with hot, crusty ciabatta or grissini sticks and a sprinkling of chili.

citrus and olive chicken on a bed of wilted wild arugula

A fabulous everyday dinner that's as good for the family as it is for guests. Removing the skin cuts loads of calories, and the stuffing ensures that none of the flavor is lost.

8 chicken pieces, bone-in, skin removed and breasts cut in half
about 20 Greek (kalamata) olives
thinly sliced peel of 1 large lemon and 1 orange

stuffing
4 fat cloves garlic, crushed
1 C mixed Italian parsley and chives, chopped
sea salt and milled black pepper
2 T olive oil

sauce
juice of 1 lemon and 1 orange
½ C chicken stock
½ C white wine
¼ C olive oil
1 t sugar
sea salt and milled black pepper
Serves 4

Make shallow slits in each chicken piece. Pit the olives and set aside. Mix the stuffing ingredients together to make a chunky paste. Push the stuffing into each slit, and rub excess stuffing over the chicken pieces.

Mix together the sauce ingredients and pour into a roasting pan. Add chicken pieces (don't do this the other way around or you'll wash off all the green bits).

Roast in a preheated 400°F oven for 20 minutes. Add olives and roast for a further 10–15 minutes. Serve sprinkled with peel on a bed of fresh arugula — the heat of the chicken and the pan juices will wilt the arugula — with couscous or garlic and olive oil mash.

citrus-roasted fish with capers

Any fish could be used for this fresh lemon-flavored dish, but salmon or yellowtail work best.

Place 4 thick fish fillets in a roasting pan. Mix together 2 T olive oil, the juice of 1 lemon, sea salt and milled black pepper and rub into fish. Very thinly slice 1 lemon and 1 orange. Place 4 overlapping citrus slices over each fish fillet (2 lemon, 2 orange). Scatter with ¼ C capers, drizzle with a little extra olive oil and bake in a preheated 400ºF oven for about 10–15 minutes, depending on the thickness of the fish. If it all looks a bit pale, pop under a preheated grill to brown. Serve with grilled zucchini ribbons and boiled or mashed potatoes.
Serves 4

sticky lime pudding

Quick, easy and immensely comforting.

This recipe is one of Australian food writer Jill Dupleix's wonderful everyday puddings — it's one of those that separates to create a soft sponge on top and a sticky lime sauce below.

2 T butter
1 C sugar
4 T plain flour, sifted
juice and grated rind of 4 ripe limes*
2 C milk
4 free-range eggs, separated**
Serves 4

Beat butter and sugar together well. Add flour, lime juice and rind. Add milk and egg yolks. Beat egg whites until stiff and fold into the mixture. Pour into a buttered ovenproof dish and bake in a preheated 350°F oven for 30–50 minutes, until the top is golden. Serve with frozen yogurt. (Don't panic when you take it out and see that the bottom is runny — this is how it's meant to be.)
*If the limes are very small, use 6 instead of 4.
**It is vital that you use fresh eggs.

As the winter chill sets in, our thoughts turn to thick, steaming bowls of soup, slow-cooked, robust-flavored stews, and glistening roasts with all the trimmings. It's time for indecently long lunches, cozy fireside dinners, and the chocolate-berry flavors of your favorite bottle of red. The shelves are groaning

winter

with earth-covered root vegetables, iron-rich parsnips perfect to roast or mash, and snow-white cauliflower just begging to be drenched in a garlicky vinaigrette. Don't wait — don your thickest socks, turn up the heat and get cooking.

parsnips

The sweet, mellow flavor of parsnips is perfect for soups, roasts and the crispiest chips.

parsnip potential

The good:
• Parsnips are a relatively good source of fiber and vitamin C.
The iffy:
• A parsnip has double the carbohydrate content of a carrot.

parsnip pointers

• It's not a good idea to peel the miniature or baby varieties, as their sweet, nutty flavor lies very near the skin. Just scrub them well, roast or braise them, and eat them whole.
• Choose smooth, small- to medium-sized, firm roots, and avoid those that are shriveled and soft. Avoid large parsnips as they often have a woody core.

short order

• Whip up a warm, **spiced soup**. Sauté leeks, parsnips, carrots and potatoes in olive oil until tender. Add chicken or vegetable stock and a pinch or two of nutmeg. Bring to the boil and simmer for 30 minutes. Blend, add a dash of milk, season and heat through.
• Coarsely mash boiled parsnips (with or without boiled carrots) with a little grated **fresh ginger**, olive oil and sea salt and milled black pepper.
• Roast sliced parsnips and whole shallots until soft and golden. Toss with mixed leaves and toasted **pecan nuts**. Dress with a mixture of thinly sliced fresh garlic, white balsamic vinegar, hazelnut oil and salt and milled black pepper.
• Parboil parsnips, slice and layer in an ovenproof dish with thinly sliced onion and thyme or **rosemary leaves**. Pour over chicken or vegetable stock and bake until soft. Serve in place of potatoes.
• Preheat oven to 350°F. Toss chunks of parsnip and **apple** into a baking tray with a few garlic cloves. Drizzle with a little olive oil, moisten with stock and add a sprinkling of sugar. Roast until cooked through. **Coarsely mash**, season with salt and pepper, and add lemon juice to taste. Toss in a handful of roughly chopped, **toasted hazelnuts**, and a handful of parsley. Serve with roast quail, pork or game.

low-fat parsnip chips

Serve with soups or as a snack with drinks.

It is best to use large parnsips for these, otherwise it becomes a little hard to handle. Scrub parsnips. Use a potato peeler to shave the parsnips into long, ribbon-like strips — there will be lots of them! Spray strips with a little olive oil spray and toss to coat. Scatter the strips onto a couple of baking trays — spread them out so the don't pile together and stay soggy. Bake in a preheated 250ºF oven for 1–1½ hours, until golden and crispy. (A fan oven will speed up proceedings, but is not essential.) Sprinkle with salt and serve. About 6 large parsnips will give you enough chips for 4 people — they're wonderful!

braised parsnips with whole-grain mustard

Peel 6 large parsnips and slice lengthwise. Blanch in boiling water for
3 minutes. Heat a little olive oil in a pan and sauté parsnips for
3 minutes. Add ½ C chicken stock, 1 heaped T whole-grain mustard and
the leaves of a small rosemary stalk. Season and slowly braise until soft
— about 15 minutes. Serve with roast meat or chicken.
Serves 4

onions

There's nothing like the smell of frying onions;
in fact, there's nothing like onions, period.

bountiful bulbs

- Onions are a rich source of carbohydrates.
- A medium-sized onion provides 46 calories.

short order

- **Slow-roasted onions**: Drizzle whole, unpeeled onions with olive oil and slow roast in a preheated 350°F oven for 1½–2 hours, basting from time to time. When soft, remove from the oven and split open. Sweet, gooey and totally delicious.
- Make **classic onion soup**. Heat a little oil in a large pot. Add 3⅓ pounds sliced onions and 3 cloves garlic and sauté over a low heat for about 30 minutes. The onions must be well browned and soft. Add thyme and bay leaf, 1¼ quarts beef stock, ½ C white wine and ¼ C medium cream sherry. Bring to a boil and simmer, covered, for about 30 minutes. Season to taste. Serve with goat cheese toasts.
- Make **glazed baby onions**: Pour boiling water over onions and leave for a few minutes to soften. Drain and place in an ovenproof dish. Mix honey, olive oil, a dash of lemon or orange juice and salt to taste, and heat gently. Pour over onions and bake at 350°F for 40–60 minutes, basting occasionally.
- Roast quartered, unpeeled onions with a selection of winter **root vegetables**, olive oil and sage and serve with your favorite roast meat.
- Make a great chunky **sweet and sour relish**. Gently cook 1 pound each pickling onions and peeled, chopped apples, 2 T raisins, 2 T balsamic or white wine vinegar, and 2 T sugar in a covered pan for 30 minutes.

sticky onion marmalade

Dollop onto sandwiches, cold meats, cheeses and anything else that strikes your fancy.

3 t olive oil
1 T brown mustard seeds
3 large onions, sliced
2 whole chilies
1 t cayenne pepper
3–4 T brown sugar
⅓ C water
¼ C red wine
2 T red wine vinegar
3 T balsamic vinegar
1 bay leaf
Makes about 2 cups

Heat olive oil in a pot and add mustard seeds. When the seeds begin to pop, add onions, chilies and cayenne pepper, and sauté for 5 minutes. Then add brown sugar and water, and cook for about 15 minutes. Add red wine, both vinegars and the bay leaf, and cook on a low heat for 15–30 minutes, until the onions have caramelized and the sauce is thick and brown. Store in a jar in the fridge and eat hot or cold. Add more chili if you want it hotter.

low-fat sausages and onions with hot mustard mash

Heat 2 T olive oil in a frying pan. Add 8 low-fat pork sausages and cook over a medium-low heat to brown on all sides — don't bother to try and get an even color, real food isn't supposed to be perfect. Remove sausages and set aside. Slice 3 onions into shells and add to the sausage juices. Cook slowly to brown — about 10–15 minutes. Add 1 heaped T whole-grain mustard and 1 C medium-cream sherry; season to taste. Return the sausages to the pan. Cover (if you don't have a lid, use a piece of foil — shiny side in) and cook over a medium heat for about 10 minutes. Give the pan a good shake from time to time to avoid any bits burning. To make the mash: cook 4–6 large, floury potatoes in lightly salted boiling water until soft. Drain and mash with 1 T olive oil and about ⅔ C low-fat or fat-free milk to get just the right consistency. Flavor with 2 T prepared hot mustard and season to taste. Serve with beet chutney.

Serves 4

cauliflower

It's made for cheese sauce,
but perhaps it's time we grew up!

cauligood stuff

• Cauliflower is high in vitamin C.

short order

• Go really simple and dress up lightly steamed, still warm cauliflower with your favorite **Italian vinaigrette**.

• Go **Asian** with 2 T peanut oil, 1 T rice wine vinegar, juice of 1 lime, a 2-inch piece of grated ginger, 1 stick finely sliced lemongrass, 1 t palm or brown sugar, 2 red chilies (sliced), 2 T water, a dash of soy sauce, salt and milled black pepper. Enough for 1 medium cauliflower.

• Blanch 2–3 C of cauliflower florets in salted, boiling water for about 5 minutes, until tender but firm. Heat 1 T olive oil in a pan, add drained and dried cauliflower and stir-fry over a high heat for about 30 seconds. Remove from heat, drizzle with lemon juice and toss with salt and milled pepper, capers, Italian parsley and grated **Parmesan**.

• Make a salad with warm, steamed cauliflower, grilled and skinned strips of red peppers, pitted **black olives** and a strong, grainy mustard and fresh chili dressing.

• Heat 1 T olive oil in a pan. Add 4 anchovies, 1 t dried chili, juice of 1 lemon and 1 T grainy mustard. Pour the **anchovy dressing** over pasta and steamed cauliflower florets. Mop up juices with crusty bread.

• Toss cooked cauliflower with peas and **crispy lean bacon**, and serve as a side dish.

• **Purée** cooked cauliflower and onion with garlic and olive oil. Season to taste and serve with roast meat.

• Go Indian and whip up a **crunchy cauliflower raita**. Heat 1 T olive oil in a pan and sauté 1 T black mustard seeds, 1 T cumin seeds, 1–2 cloves crushed garlic and 1 sliced red pepper until aromatic — about 2–3 minutes. Coat 2 C florets with spices, add a bit of water and cook until tender. Cool and stir in about $^1/_2$ C low-fat yogurt. Season and serve as an accompaniment to an Indian meal.

cauliflower and anchovy winter salad

This is a sort of cauliflower Niçoise — serve as a light lunch or as a side salad with roast chicken.

9–14 ounces cauliflower florets
9 ounces green beans, tailed
12 baby potatoes, halved
2–3 boiled eggs, halved
4–6 anchovy fillets, sliced lengthwise
3 T olive oil
juice of ½ lemon
2 T water
1 fat clove garlic, finely chopped
1 t sugar
1 t mustard powder
1 ounce chives, finely chopped
sea salt and milled black pepper
Serves 4 as a side salad

Steam cauliflower florets and green beans. Boil potatoes. Toss cooked vegetables and eggs in a bowl with the anchovies. Make a dressing with the remaining ingredients. Pour dressing over vegetable mixture and serve while still warm.

Indian spiced cauliflower and potatoes

Serve as a side dish or as a main course with rice and sambals.

Heat 1 T olive oil in a pot; add 1 sliced onion, 3 cloves crushed garlic and 2 t grated ginger, and cook, over a low heat, to brown. Add 1 t black mustard seeds and cook over a medium heat, until the seeds begin to pop. Add 1 T ground cumin, 1 t tumeric and 1 t crushed dried chili flakes. Cook to release aroma — about 2 minutes. Add 1 pound halved new potatoes and stir-fry over a low heat for about 5 minutes. Add vegetable stock (2 C in total), a little at a time, to prevent potatoes from sticking. When potatoes begin to soften, add 1 cauliflower, broken into florets (about 5 C). Toss to coat and slightly brown. Add remaining stock, sugar, 10 fresh curry leaves, a squeeze of lemon juice and 1 t salt. Cover and cook until vegetables are tender. Stir in a handful of chopped fresh coriander and serve. Serves 4

soup-erb

One of the best things about winter is slow-cooked, flavor-packed soups. There's nothing more comforting than a steaming bowl to shrug off the chill — and if the soup is also low in fat but hearty enough to fill you up, so much the better!

detox soup

A powerful detoxifying vegetable combination that you just know is doing you good.

2 T olive oil
2 t garlic, crushed
1 large onion or 2 well-washed leeks, chopped
4 sticks celery, chopped
4 carrots, sliced
2 large handfuls chopped cabbage
about 5 ounces (½ bag) spinach, spines removed, shredded
a large handful of parsley, roughly chopped
1½ quarts vegetable stock
1 x 14-ounce can whole peeled tomatoes, roughly chopped
sea salt and milled black pepper
Serves 4

Heat oil in a large, deep pot and fry garlic for 2 minutes. Add onions or leeks, celery and carrots and cook for 5 minutes, until soft. Add cabbage, spinach and parsley and toss to mix well. Add stock, tomatoes and seasoning. Bring to a boil, and reduce heat. Simmer for 30–40 minutes and enjoy as a snack or for lunch or dinner.
Note: You can cut out the fat altogether — simply toss all the ingredients into the pot and cook!

soup success

• If making your own stock is a little beyond your culinary abilities, opt for cartons of fresh stock or use MSG-free stock powder mixed with water.

• Soup parties are a wonderful and inexpensive way to entertain in winter. Rustle up 2 large pots of different soup, buy at least 3 types of bread and ask your friends to bring the odd wedge of cheese. Add a couple of bottles of wine, light every candle in the house, batten down the hatches and have fun.

• While puréed soups can be delicious, they are best as part of a meal rather than the meal itself — so go chunky and rustic for soup and bread suppers.

• Cut calories and sauté ingredients in stock instead of oil, or use olive oil spray.

• I always try and make double quantities of soup. It freezes well (unless it includes potatoes, which tend to go spongy) and lasts for at least a week in the fridge, making after-work snacks or late suppers instant, stress-free and totally delicious.

fresh tomato and basil soup

One of my all-time favorites — the secret is in adding the garlic and fresh basil at the end of the cooking time.

2 T olive oil
1 large onion, chopped
1 large carrot, peeled and grated
1 stalk celery with leaves, chopped
4 cloves garlic, crushed
1 x 14-ounce can whole peeled tomatoes, chopped, juice retained
6 large ripe tomatoes, peeled and chopped
½ t sugar
3 C chicken or vegetable stock, made with 1½ t stock powder
a handful of fresh basil, chopped
sea salt and milled black pepper
Serves 4

Heat oil in a large saucepan. Add onion, carrot, celery and ¼ of the garlic, and sauté until soft — about 5–7 minutes. Add tomatoes (with juice), sugar, seasoning and stock, and bring to a boil. Reduce heat, cover and simmer for 30–40 minutes. Remove from heat, add basil and remaining garlic and adjust seasoning. Serve with crusty bread and cheese, like fat-free Philadelphia.
Note: You can bulk up the soup with a can or two of drained cannellini beans or 1 C macaroni.

chicken noodle soup

For body and soul.

½ chicken, skinned
2 T olive oil
1 onion, diced
4 sticks celery, diced
4 carrots, diced
2 cloves garlic, sliced
2½ quarts good chicken stock
milled black pepper
2 bay leaves
½ pound long, thin egg noodles,
    broken in half, or small soup pasta
    in different shapes
Serves 4

Cut the chicken into large chunks. Heat oil in a large pot and sauté onion, celery, carrots and garlic for 5–7 minutes, until softened. Add the chicken pieces, including bones. Pour in stock, season with pepper, and add bay leaves. Bring to a boil, reduce heat and simmer for about 45 minutes. If you don't want the bones in the soup, remove them at this stage. Add the noodles and cook until done. Adjust seasoning, and serve.

Note: If you feel the chunks of chicken are too big, shred them further before adding the noodles. Save calories — omit the oil and simply boil all the ingredients together.

beef, barley and pumpkin soup

The meat simply provides the flavor,
so bones could be used instead.

⅔–1 pound beef shin
flour for dusting
1 T olive oil
1 onion, chopped
1–2 cloves garlic, sliced
about 5 ounces (medium wedge) pumpkin,
  peeled and chopped, seeds removed
2 whole, fresh chilies
1 t ground paprika
2 potatoes, peeled and quartered
12 ounces zucchini, trimmed and thickly sliced
1 C barley or brown rice
1½ quarts beef stock (1 t stock powder, heaped,
  mixed with boiling water)
½ C dry white wine
1 t sugar
sea salt and milled black pepper
Serves 4–6

Dust beef with a little flour and shake to remove
excess. Heat oil in a large pot and gently brown the
meat. Add onion and garlic and sauté for a minute
or two. Add remaining ingredients, except courgettes, and bring to a boil. Reduce heat, cover and
simmer for about 30 minutes. Add courgettes and
simmer for a further 20 minutes.

bean, lentil and spinach soup

Filling and fabulous!

Heat 2 T olive oil in a large pot. Add 2 peeled, chopped onions, 1 clove crushed garlic and 1 t ground cumin, and sauté for 3 minutes. Add 2 peeled, chopped carrots, 9 ounces brown lentils, 1 can each of rinsed and drained cannellini and kidney beans, 2 T tomato purée (not paste), 1 quart vegetable stock (made with 1½ t stock powder), sea salt and milled black pepper. Bring to a boil, reduce heat, cover and simmer for 30–40 minutes. Add about 11 ounces roughly chopped spinach leaves and a large handful chopped Italian parsley. Adjust seasoning and cook for a further 10 minutes. Serves 4

raring to roast

A succulent, home-cooked roast is the ultimate winter comfort. It's simple to prepare, healthier than you think, and the last word in delicious.

lemon and herb roast chicken

The flavor of a free-range chicken is far superior to that of a caged chicken — so spend the extra money and taste the difference.

1 large free-range chicken, about 3⅓ pounds
juice of 2 small lemons
½ C basil or sage, roughly chopped
½ C Italian parsley, roughly chopped
2 cloves garlic, crushed
1 T olive oil
sea salt and milled black pepper
Serves 4

Preheat oven to 400ºF. Wash the cavity of the chicken well and shake to dry. Squeeze the juice of one lemon into the cavity and season well. Mix together herbs, garlic, olive oil and seasoning. Gently lift the skin at the tip of the chicken breasts. Use your fingertips to separate the skin and membrane from the meat of the breast. Push in the herb mixture. Place the chicken in a roasting pan, squeeze over juice of the other lemon. Drizzle with a little extra olive oil and rub into the skin. Season well. Tie the legs together with string — this is not entirely necessary, as you're not stuffing the bird, but it does look a little more, um, genteel! Pop into the oven and roast for about 90 minutes. A smaller bird, say under 3 pounds, should take about 1 hour to cook. Rest for 10 minutes before carving.

Note: For a super-moist bird, but without crispy skin, place the chicken on a rack in the roasting pan and pour over 2 C chicken stock — the chicken sort of roasts and steams at the same time — great for sandwiches and salads.

spiced beef fillet

The Middle Eastern flavors of cumin and coriander work particularly well with beef.

4½ pounds good-quality beef or fillet
2 T olive oil
1 T each ground cumin and coriander
3 cloves garlic, crushed
½ T dried chili flakes
sea salt and milled black pepper
Serves 6–8

Preheat oven to 400°F. Tie beef with string to keep its shape — not critical, but it does make for a neater result. Rub fillet with a little olive oil. Mix remaining ingredients together and spread over a flat surface. Roll fillet in spices to coat evenly. Heat a large, non-stick pan over a high heat. Add a splash of oil and sear fillet on all sides to brown. Transfer meat to a baking dish and pop into the oven. Roast for 25–30 minutes for rare, or longer, as desired. Remove from oven, cover with foil and allow to rest for 10 minutes before carving.
Note: Ignore everything else you've ever read and when cooking fillet. Work on about 8 minutes per pound — you can always cook it a bit longer if it's too bloody, but it's difficult to save a gray, dried-out fillet.

aromatic pork roast

Low-fat pork loin can be succulent and delicious, as long as you don't overcook it. Oriental flavors give it a modern twist.

Preheat oven to 375ºF. Place a 4–4½-pound boneless, rolled pork loin in a roasting pan. Mix together 2 T brown sugar, ½ C low-sodium soy sauce, 2 t dried chili flakes, 3 cloves crushed garlic, 2 T freshly grated ginger, 2 t Chinese 5-spice powder, the juice of 2 limes and the grated peel of 1 orange. Season to taste. Pour over pork and marinate for at least 1 hour. Pop into the oven and roast for 30 minutes. Reduce heat to 325ºF and roast for a further 15–20 minutes, basting frequently. Remove from oven, cover with foil and allow to rest for 10–20 minutes before carving.
Serves 6–8

sunshine roast vegetables

Dense, textured orange and yellow vegetables are great for roasting, and their sunshine colors brighten any winter meal.

10 baby carrots, with stalks
10 baby parsnips, scrubbed
about 6 potatoes, skin on, cut into large chunks
2 large onions, skin on, cut into wedges
3 C butternut chunks, skin on, seeds removed
8 cloves unpeeled garlic
2 T freshly grated ginger
2 T olive oil
2 whole red chilies
1 T brown sugar
juice of 1 orange
sea salt and milled black pepper
Serves 4–6

Preheat oven to 350°F. Place all ingredients in a roasting pan. Use your hands and toss all the ingredients to coat well. Place in the oven and roast for 40–60 minutes, until vegetables are soft and golden. Give them a good shake from time to time.

twice as nice

Don't toss out your leftovers or (eek, how boring) dish up the same meal two days in a row — go gourmet and give 'em a twist. Here's how.

spiced yogurt lamb

Leftover roast lamb makes the most wonderful Turkish-inspired dish.

1 T olive oil
1 onion, thinly sliced
2 cloves garlic, crushed
1 t minced ginger
2 t ground cumin
2 t ground coriander
1 t paprika
2 t dried chili flakes
2 C leftover lamb cut into
    medium-thick strips
2 T water
squeeze of lemon juice, about 1 T
¾ C fat-free yogurt
a large handful (3 T) fresh coriander, chopped
sea salt and milled black pepper
Serves 2 generously

Heat olive oil in a pan and cook onion over medium heat to lightly brown. Add garlic, ginger and spices, and cook for a minute or two, until fragrant. Add lamb and toss to coat with spices. Add water and lemon juice, and cook for a minute. Add yogurt and cook over a low heat for 5 minutes. The yogurt will curdle if the heat is too intense. Don't panic if this happens — it will look a little odd but taste just fine. Add coriander, adjust seasoning and serve with hot pita bread, chopped tomatoes, onion and cucumber and a few fresh leaves.

Thai beef salad

Usually the beef is cooked specifically for this dish so that it is warm, but I often make it with leftover beef and it tastes just as good.

¼ C brown rice, uncooked
about 1 pound (2–2½ C) rare beef (rump, sirloin or
  fillet), sliced into strips
juice of 1¼ limes
4 T fish sauce
2 red or green chilies, finely sliced
1 T ginger, peeled and sliced into matchsticks
1 T brown or palm sugar
3 T water
a generous handful (3 T) mint, finely chopped
2 T coriander, chopped
1 red onion or 1 bunch green onions, sliced on
  the slant
milled black pepper
Serves 2

Heat a dry pan; add rice and toast for 4–5 minutes, until it begins to pop. Keep a vigilant eye out, or it will burn. Remove and toss into a bowl with sliced beef. Combine remaining ingredients, except herbs and green onions, in a small pot and heat gently to warm through. Pour dressing over beef and rice, add herbs and green onion and serve.

chicken and vegetable soup

Harness the carcass and the leftover bits of meat for a fabulously comforting, fat-free chicken and vegetable soup.

2 large onions, chopped
4–6 carrots, peeled and sliced
2 leeks, washed and chopped
4 stalks celery, with most of the leaves, chopped
2 cloves garlic, sliced
1 leftover chicken carcass, skin removed, with pan juices and "bits"
2 fresh or dried bay leaves
1 t sugar
sea salt and milled black pepper
2½ quarts chicken stock (made with 1 heaped T stock powder)
a handful (3 T) Italian parsley, roughly chopped
Serves 4

Place chopped vegetables in a large pot. Add the chicken carcass, any of the congealed pan juices and leftover meat, skin removed. Add the bay leaves, sugar and seasoning, and pour over stock. Bring to a boil, reduce heat, cover and simmer for about 1½ hours. Remove carcass, season, add parsley and cook for a further 5 minutes.

Note: You could also make a real chicken stock, instead of a soup — use half of the amount of vegetables and replace the stock with water. Cook, strain and use as the base for soups and Asian dishes.

salmon kedgeree

There are tons of things you can do with leftover rice. This is one of the nicest — and it's suitable for breakfast, lunch and dinner. Substitute fresh fish with chunks of canned pink salmon if you like. A word of warning: Use rice within two days, or freeze it. Don't panic at the list of ingredients, the method's dead easy!

2 fillets fresh fish of your choice
2 bay leaves
1 T olive oil
½ T black mustard seeds
1 large onion or 1 bunch green onions, finely chopped
1 clove garlic, finely sliced
1 T good-quality, medium-strength curry powder
1 t turmeric
6–8 fresh or dried curry leaves
3 C cooked basmati rice
¼ C baby tomatoes or 2 tomatoes, seeded and cut into chunks
2 t lemon juice
¼ C stock (made with 1 t chicken or vegetable stock powder)
1 t sugar
sea salt and milled black pepper
a handful fresh coriander, roughly chopped
2 boiled eggs, peeled and quartered
Serves 2

Place fish and bay leaves in a shallow pan and add water to just cover. Bring to a boil and simmer for about 5 minutes. Remove from pan, allow to cool, and flake gently. Heat olive oil in a large pan. Add mustard seeds and cook until they begin to pop. Add onion and garlic and sauté for about 4 minutes over a medium heat until soft and translucent. Sprinkle in curry powder, turmeric and curry leaves, and cook until fragrant. Stir in rice, tomatoes, lemon juice, stock and sugar and toss to coat well. Season well and gently stir in flaked fish. Cook to heat through, garnish with fresh coriander and quartered eggs. Serve with chopped, fresh chili and a dollop of yogurt.

Breeze into the bright, warm days of spring,
cheerful, crisp colors and the happy smell of new life that fills the
air. Tender stems of asparagus and sweet, sugary peppers add
new crunch to pastas and salads, pale green avocados make

spring

toast a creamy treat, and tiny jasmine blossoms creep through
open windows. Bees buzz, dinners move outdoors and glasses
tinkle in the fresh wave of sundowners.

asparagus

Asparagus can lend an air of luxury and
hedonism to even the most staid occasions.

asparagus assets

Asparagus is the young shoot of a leafless plant that comes from the lily family. It has a myriad of health benefits:

• It's known to be a great diuretic — it contains an alkaloid called asparagine, which stimulates the kidneys.
• Contains vitamins C and A, the latter being more prevalent in the green variety.
• Also contains folic acid, which is one of the B vitamins.

the art of asparagus

• The three most common types of asparagus are: green (with the slightly purple tips); thick, woody white spears; and spue, very thin green asparagus, which are great raw.
• Some of the thicker green asparagus can be quite tough and stringy at the bottom. Use a potato peeler to shave off the outer skin at the base of the stem.
• White asparagus tends to have a tough skin until quite near the tip. Peel as you need to.
• The best way to cook green asparagus is to part boil, part steam them. Tie the asparagus in bundles. Place into a deep pot with enough boiling water to reach ¼ way up the asparagus. Cover and boil until cooked. This way, the tougher parts get to boil while the more delicate tips steam.
• Asparagus can be stir-fried or roasted from raw, but for quiches or bakes, lightly blanch, then use as directed.

short order

• Steam fresh green asparagus. Drain well and serve drizzled with extra virgin olive oil and lashings of **Parmesan** shavings.
• Lightly steamed asparagus, wrap in prosciutto ham, roll in **phyllo dough** and bake until golden brown and crisp.
• Sauté in garlic and olive oil and toss into your favorite **fresh pasta**. Serve with lots of freshly grated Parmesan.
• Steam asparagus and serve as part of a salad with boiled baby potatoes, **smoked salmon** and a lemony vinaigrette dressing.
• Fold into creamy **scrambled eggs** and salmon; or use for dipping into a soft-boiled egg.
• Wrap with thin slices of **prosciutto** or smoked salmon and serve with cocktails.
• Sauté in a little vegetable stock with mint and **fresh peas** and serve with roast chicken or fish.

grilled asparagus with prosciutto and basil

Three of the world's best flavors on one plate!

½ pound fresh green asparagus
olive oil spray
½ C fresh basil leaves, roughly chopped
2 T olive oil
1 T balsamic vinegar
sea salt and milled pepper
8 slices good quality prosciutto ham
Serves 4

Blanch asparagus in boiling water for a minute. Refresh in cold water and drain. Spray a grill pan with olive oil spray and heat till smoking. Cook asparagus until tender. Meanwhile mix basil, olive oil, balsamic vinegar and seasoning together. Arrange asparagus in bundles and loosely wrap in prosciutto Ham. Place on a large plate and drizzle with basil mixture. Serve with hot crusty bread.

asparagus, dill and pea pasta

1½C chicken or vegetable stock (1 t stock powder), ½ pound asparagus, halved, 1 C fresh peas, 1 T olive oil, 2 T fresh dill, sea salt and milled pepper, ½ pound fresh pasta.

Serves 4 as a starter; 2 as a generous main dish.

Place stock in a large pan and bring to a boil. Add asparagus and peas and cook until tender, about 6 minutes. Add oil and dill and season to taste. Cook pasta until al dente. Stir asparagus mixture into drained pasta and serve with freshly shaved Parmasan cheese.

peppers

Raw, roasted, char-grilled or stuffed, these rainbow-colored delights are as healthy as they are versatile and delicious.

in praise of peppers

• Peppers (also known as bell or sweet peppers) are part of the capsicum family, along with chilies. They all start off green and change color according to ripeness and variety. The entire capsicum family is rich in vitamin C — even more so than citrus fruit. Foods rich in vitamin C enhance the absorption of iron.

• Peppers also contain the antioxidant beta carotene.

short order

• **Stuff peppers** with spicy lentils and rice. Cook brown rice and/or lentils in vegetable stock. Meanwhile, cut the tops off peppers, scoop out seeds and rub with a little oil. Place a little water in a roasting pan, add peppers and grill until just softened — about 8 minutes. Fry onion and garlic with ground cumin, coriander and **chili flakes**, toss in rice and/or lentils and cook to incorporate flavors. Add a handful of chopped **fresh tomatoes**, a few fresh herbs and a bit of crumbled feta, and stuff into pepper cavities. Bake in a preheated 350°F oven to heat through.

• Whip up Italian-style **grilled peppers**. Halve a pepper, seed it and place under a hot grill. Cook to blacken skins. Pop into a plastic bag for about 15 minutes; the skin will sweat and come away. Remove skin and thickly slice the flesh into strips. Drizzle with olive oil and balsamic vinegar, season and use in salads and **pasta sauces**; on sandwiches or as part of an antipasto table.

• Cut into chunks and cook slowly with garlic, tomatoes, a hint of chili and a bit of sugar. Season well and, when ready to serve, add fresh herbs, chopped **anchovies**, pitted black olives, or all of the above. Serve as a pasta sauce or drizzle over pan-fried chicken breasts or **grilled fish**.

• Stir-fry pepper in a little olive oil until just soft. Add a good glug of **sweet chili sauce** and a squeeze of lime juice. Cook over a high heat to slightly caramelize, add a handful of fresh basil or **coriander** and serve as a relish on sandwiches or with grilled meat.

spiced masala omelette

Indian breakfast at its best — or serve this as a light supper with steamed basmati rice and a dollop of chili sauce.

4 t peanut or canola oil
3 spring onions, finely sliced
1 red or yellow pepper, finely chopped
1–2 green chilies, finely chopped
1 clove garlic, crushed
2 t garam masala
2 t ground cumin
sea salt and milled black pepper
4 free-range or omega-3 enriched eggs, lightly
    beaten
Serves 2

Heat 2 t of the oil in a non-stick pan. Add spring onions, sliced pepper, chili and garlic, and stir-fry for about 2 minutes. Add spices and cook for a further 1 minute. Remove mixture and set aside. Heat remaining oil in the same pan. Add egg and cook, agitating with a fork from time to time. When the egg is *just* set, scatter the reserved mixture over half of the omelette and flip to create a half-moon shape. Serve with fresh coriander.

Thai-style baked fish

Impressive to look at and fabulous to eat. Preheat oven to 400ºF.
Score a 4 ½-pound white-fleshed fish on both sides and tuck a
few basil leaves into the cuts. Loosely wrap fish in 2 large sheets
of foil, shiny side in. Seal the edges, but leave enough room for air
to circulate while the fish cooks. Place fish on a baking tray and
bake for about 30–50 minutes, depending on the size of the fish.
Dressing: Place into a pot 4 T fish sauce, 3 T fresh lime or lemon
juice,1 T palm or brown sugar, 1 fat clove crushed garlic, a
2-inch piece of fresh ginger, peeled and cut into matchsticks, 1
bunch fresh, chopped coriander, 2 red chilies, seeded and finely
sliced, ½ cucumber and 2 carrots, cut into thin matchsticks, and
1 red or yellow pepper, seeded and finely sliced. Bring to a boil
and immediately remove from heat. Season to taste. Transfer fish
to platter and pour over vegetable dressing while still hot. Serve
with steamed jasmine or basmati rice.
Serves 4–6

avocados

Good for you, versatile and just plain yummy,
avocados are nature's own wonder food.

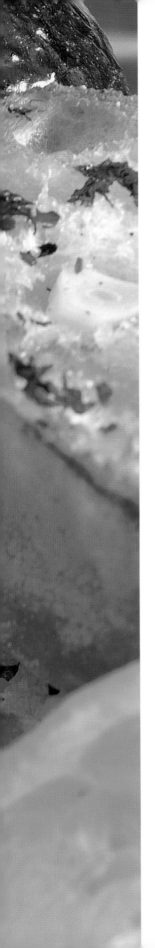

avo advantages

- The poor avocado has been given bad press for a long time due to its high calorie count and fat content — ouch! But the fat they contain is mono-unsaturated, the same healthy fat found in olive oil.
- Avocados are a source of potassium (more so than bananas) and are also rich in vitamin E.
- Avocado oil, extracted from the pit, is almost flavorless and colorless. It's great in salad dressings made with white wine vinegar.

avo tips

- If you are only using half an avocado, leave the pit in the unused half, wrap it in plastic and refrigerate; this will prevent discoloration.
- Brush exposed flesh with lemon, lime juice or vinegar to stop it from turning brown.
- If you have made an avocado purée and are not going to use it straight away, place it in a sealed plastic container, with the pit.
- The test for ripeness is the same for all types of avocados — it should be yielding at the stalk end, should not be too soft, and the skin shouldn't be broken, discolored or brown.
- To ripen avocados, store at room temperature in a brown paper bag. To speed up the ripening process, place avos in a bowl alongside bananas.

short order

- Mash together avocado, **feta**, lemon juice and milled black pepper. Stir in a few chopped green onions and some sliced, pickled peppers and pile into crispy **baked potatoes**.
- Pile uncooked chopped avo onto your **favorite pizza** after it's been baked.
- Fill **omelettes** with avo, sautéed baby tomatoes and a little crumbled feta.
- Whip up a simple **salad** — marinate thick slices of ripe tomato in olive oil, garlic, salt and a dash of balsamic vinegar. Serve topped with chunks of ripe avocado, on crusty bread.
- Make a Caribbean-style **salsa** with small chunks of avocado and papaya, tossed with finely chopped **red onion**, lime juice, garlic, chili and coriander. Season well and add sugar to taste. Serve with grilled fish or chicken.
- Toss **butter lettuce** with lemon juice and olive oil and add bits of crispy, low-fat turkey bacon and chunks of avocado. Add a few **green onions** for texture and serve with crusty bread for a **light and easy lunch**.

roasted red onion, arugula and avocado salad

Serve on its own with crusty bread, or as part of a meal with roast lamb or chicken and baby boiled potatoes.

4 medium red onions
2 T olive oil
2 T balsamic vinegar
1 t brown sugar
3 fat cloves garlic, thinly sliced
2 C water
2 ounces arugula leaves, well washed
1 butter lettuce
1 large avocado, peeled, quartered and cut into chunks
sea salt and milled black pepper

dressing
1 T tahini
juice of 1 lemon
2 T water
1 clove garlic, crushed
1 T olive oil
1 t brown sugar
a handful fresh basil, chopped
salt and milled black pepper
Serves 4

Peel onions without removing the hairy stalk end (this keeps the onion together). Quarter and place in a roasting pan. Mix together oil, vinegar, sugar, garlic and water. Season and pour over onions. Roast in a preheated 400°F oven for about 30 minutes, until onions are soft and caramelized. Remove and set aside. Toss arugula leaves, lettuce and avocado. Whisk dressing ingredients together in a bowl and toss over leaves. Add onions, toss to combine, and serve.

lemon and avocado linguine

It makes a world of difference using fresh pasta instead of dried with the subtle flavor of these ingredients. If you do opt for dried pasta, use something very delicate, like angel hair pasta.

Cook 1 pound fresh pasta according to package instructions. Meanwhile, heat 3 T olive oil in a small pot. Add 2 fat cloves crushed garlic, the finely sliced peel of 1 lemon, and 1 small red chili (optional), seeded and chopped. Cook for about 2 minutes. Add 3 T fresh lemon juice and 4 T vegetable stock, and season to taste. Cook for another minute and remove from heat. Drain pasta and toss with the flesh of 2 firm, ripe chopped avocados, and about 16 pitted and halved Greek (kalamata) olives. Serve immediately. Serves 4

sunshine food

Big flavors and bright colors are the
essence of this season's sunshine foods.

slow-roasted tomatoes on herbed couscous

3 fat cloves garlic, thinly sliced
1 t sugar
3 T olive oil
2 T balsamic vinegar
sea salt and milled black pepper
4 plum tomatoes, halved lengthways
12 small tomatoes

couscous

1 T olive oil
1 small onion, chopped
1 celery stick, finely sliced
2 zucchinis, chopped
1 fresh chili, very finely chopped
2 C couscous
2 C boiling vegetable stock or water
a handful Italian parsley, roughly chopped
Serves 4

Mix together garlic, sugar, oil, vinegar and seasoning. Place larger tomatoes, cut side up, on a baking tray; drizzle with oil and vinegar mixture. Place on the second shelf from the bottom in a preheated 300°F oven. Roast for 35 minutes, or until soft and squishy, but still holding their shape. Add small tomatoes and the rest of the dressing, and roast for a further 10 minutes.

Meanwhile, make the couscous. Heat oil in a pot. Add onion and sauté for 2–3 minutes. Add celery, zucchini and chili, and cook until just tender — about 5 minutes. Add couscous and quickly toss to coat. Pour over water or stock, and immediately cover with a lid. Cook for 30 seconds and remove from heat. Leave to steam for 10 minutes. Remove lid, add parsley and fluff with a fork to mix well and separate grains.

To serve, pile couscous into heated bowls and spoon over tomatoes and their roasting juices. Good with freshly shaved Parmesan.

blackened salmon with roasted red pepper and chili drizzle

dressing
1 red pepper
2 jalapeño or other mild red chilies
2 fat cloves garlic
¼ C olive oil
1 T balsamic vinegar
sea salt and milled black pepper

salmon
4 salmon fillets, skin on
olive oil
2 t paprika
3 cloves garlic, crushed
½ t sugar
sea salt and milled black pepper
Serves 4

Preheat grill. Halve pepper and chilies, remove seeds and pith. Place on a baking tray skin side up, toss in unpeeled garlic, and grill to char and blacken flesh (the garlic should only soften slightly). Remove blackened skin and finely chop flesh. Peel garlic and crush or finely chop. Mix together with remaining dressing ingredients and set aside until needed.

Brush salmon with oil. Mix paprika, garlic, sugar and seasoning and rub into salmon flesh. Heat a heavy, non-stick frying pan until smoking. Add the salmon, flesh side down, and sear without moving for 2 minutes. Turn and cook for a further 3–4 minutes, depending on the thickness — the salmon should be slightly undercooked, opaque, moist and juicy. Remove skin and flake salmon into large chunks. Place on 4 plates, and drizzle with roasted pepper and chili dressing.

*As an alternative, serve the salmon on a bed of salad leaves and cucumber ribbons, or on thick slices of crusty ciabatta.

boozy plums in red wine and port

Fat-free and decadent.

1 C port
½ C red wine
½ C water
½ C sugar
peel of 1 orange
juice of 1 lemon
8–10 plums
Serves 4

Place port, wine, water, sugar and peel in a pot and bring to a boil. Reduce heat and simmer for 10 minutes. Add plums, whole or halved as preferred, and cook gently for 20–25 minutes. Allow plums to cool in the syrup. Serve as is or with fat-free yogurt flavored with honey.

warm beef and roasted asparagus salad

Place 1 pound mature rump in a shallow container. Mix 4 cloves sliced garlic, the juice of 2 large lemons, 2 T olive oil and 1 T whole-grain mustard together. Season with milled black pepper and pour over steak. Allow to marinate for at least 30 minutes. Preheat oven to 400°F. Place 7 ounces green asparagus on a baking tray and drizzle with a little olive oil, lemon juice and sea salt. Roast for 10–15 minutes. (They must still be green and slightly crunchy.) Meanwhile, spray a grill pan with olive oil spray and heat until smoking. Cook steak. Remove from pan; allow to rest for 5 minutes. Pour any reserved marinade juices into a small bowl and add 1 t lemon juice, ½ t sugar and 1 T olive oil. Mix well and drizzle over a selection of your favorite mixed herbs and salad leaves. Season well. Slice steak. Arrange leaves, a small handful of roasted asparagus and a few slices of steak on individual plates. Serve with crusty bread or hot, boiled potatoes.
Serves 4

grilled salmon with
bacon and mushroom
spiked barley

go with the grain

Here it is: everything you ever needed to know about grains.

grain basics

• All grains have three things in common — an outer covering (the inedible husk and nutrient-rich bran); the endosperm, which is the bulk of the edible part of the kernel containing starch and proteins and the largest part of the grain; and the germ, which is the nutrient-rich inner part of the grain. Whole grain is milled in its entirety (except for the husk) and therefore contains all the goodness.

• Whole grains are a good source of most of the B vitamins and fiber. There are two types of fiber: water-insoluble fiber and water-soluble fiber. Whole grains are a good source of water-insoluble fiber that swells like a sponge and helps evacuate … er … waste matter and reduce the risk of certain diseases, such as cancer and heart disease. The water-soluble fiber found in oats, legumes and fruits and vegetables assists in lowering cholesterol levels. Fiber also helps make one feel fuller for longer.

barley

One of the most ancient cultivated grains, barley has many uses. Malted barley is used for brewing and distilling. Whole-grain barley is used in Scots barley broth and lamb dishes, or sprouted for use in salads. Pearl barley is a more polished, refined grain that cooks faster and is great to add to soups for both thickening and flavoring.

Barley flour has a low gluten content, and is used in baking mixtures and for thickening sauces and soups. Barley is rich in phosphorous, magnesium and B vitamins, and also contains calcium and iron. It also reportedly has a soothing effect on the intestines.

Barley water, made with pearled barley and citrus extracts, is used as a skin-beautifying drink.

cooking

Boil 1 part barley with 3 parts water for 3 minutes. Reduce heat and simmer until the liquid has been absorbed and the grains are soft.

short order

• Stir spinach, grilled **lean bacon and sautéed mushrooms** into cooked barley, and serve with grilled salmon or chicken breasts.

• Toss with other grains and rice to create a **nutty side dish** to a main meal.

• Toss into your favorite chicken, vegetable or meat-based **soup**.

• Add **sprouted** barley to salads or stir-fries.

pearled whole-wheat bread

pearled whole wheat

Nutty and delicious, this grain is used in whole-wheat bread, either ground as flour or in the whole-kernel form. It makes a great, healthy salad or a fiber-packed, hot side dish. The husk provides protein, vitamins and minerals — phosphorous, potassium and iron. The germ contains large amounts of vitamins B and E, as well as minerals, protein and oil. The endosperm, the largest part of the grain, is mostly made up of starch and protein, and is used to make white flour.

The vitamin B in whole-wheat keeps the digestive tract functioning, improves our ability to cope with stress and depression, and guards against skin problems, like boils and acne. Vitamin E helps to keep the reproductive system healthy and ensures proper circulation. Sprouting the grain, by the way, doubles the vitamin B content and increases the vitamin C by around 6 times.

cooking
Use 1 part whole wheat to 2 parts water. Bring to a boil and simmer until the grains are soft.

short order
• Soak it, and toss into your **favorite bread** recipe for a health hit and a whole lot of texture.
• It mixes well with other grains like **rice, barley** or **millet**, and increases their protein value.
• Cook, cool and toss with chopped celery, **ripe tomatoes**, capers, goat or feta cheese and torn basil leaves. Drizzle with white balsamic vinegar, olive oil and garlic dressing.
• Simply boil and serve hot, seasoned with sea salt and drizzled with **olive oil**.
• Whip up a sort of **pilaf** with sautéed onions and garlic; add fresh and/or roasted vegetables, season and stir-fry until just cooked. Add cooked pearled whole wheat.

bulgur (cracked wheat)

This nutty grain is most commonly associated with Lebanese food, and most particularly their famous tabbouleh salad. The wheat grain has been parcooked to split (crack) the grain, and so absorbs moisture readily and cooks faster. A very healthy alternative to rice or potatoes, packed with fiber and vitamins B and E.

cooking
Cover 1 part grain in 2 parts salted, boiling water. Cover and allow to stand for about 20 minutes.

short order
• Whip up a **tabbouleh salad**: Soak and drain bulgur, and marinate in lemon juice, garlic and mint for 30 minutes. Chop tomatoes, cucumber, olives, spring onions and mint, and add to bulgur. Drizzle with olive oil and season to taste. Chopped peppers, red onion and feta cheese are not traditional additions, but taste great all the same.

• Sauté onion, garlic and herbs in olive oil; add chopped red pepper, mushrooms, nuts and seeds. Stir in prepared bulgur. **Stuff vegetables** or chicken with the mixture and roast.

• Serve hot or cold as is, or mix with **legumes** like chickpeas or lentils and serve in place of rice or mash.

• Bulgur works well with the **Oriental flavors** of ginger, garlic, spring onions and soy sauce.

• Prepare and cool. Sauté onions, garlic, **dried chili flakes**, peppers and herbs until just cooked. Add diced, cooked meat or chicken and bulgur.

tomato-scented couscous salad

COUSCOUS

Couscous, a staple food of North Africa, is fine golden semolina made from the first milling of durum wheat, the hardest wheat grown. The semolina is rolled, dampened and coated with finer wheat flour, which enlarges the grain and keeps it separate when cooking. Because it's made from fine, yellow durum wheat, it has a higher protein and gluten content than products made from soft wheat. And, because it's been processed, the nutritional content is not as beneficial as whole grains — but it's delicious all the same.

cooking

• Commercially produced couscous simply needs the grains to be moistened and then steamed to expand. Cover 1 part couscous with 1 part boiling water or stock. Add salt and a dash of oil. Cover with a tight-fitting lid. Cook for 30 seconds and remove from heat. Do not remove lid; allow to stand for 10 minutes. Fluff with a fork. Drizzle with olive oil.

• There is a special pot called a couscoussiere, which allows couscous to be steamed above whatever you're cooking, absorbing the aromas.

short order

• Use as a **stuffing for roast chicken**, or better still, baby chickens. Cover with boiling water to moisten but do not allow to steam. Mix with herbs, garlic, orange and lemon juice, nuts and raisins. Stuff into the cavity of a chicken and roast as usual.

• Use as you would rice. Cook with stock or water and serve as is, or stir in roasted or steamed vegetables, **roasted nuts** and fresh herbs.

• Use tomato juice, tomato pulp, vinegar and seasoning in place of water to create **tomato-scented couscous**. Toss in chopped herbs, olives or any of your favorite salad ingredients for a crunchy lunch-time treat.

• Stuff large, ripe tomatoes, **peppers** or **eggplant** with cooked couscous, mushrooms, nuts and mint. Pour over a dressing of tomato pulp, olive oil, garlic and lemon juice, and bake until heated through.

• Serve with **Moroccan-style** roast or hearty stews.

polenta

The Italian name for fine, golden cornmeal. Cornmeal is a staple throughout the world, providing a high-energy meal, rich in carbohydrates, fats and proteins. Yellow cornmeal contains more nutrients than white, is rich in magnesium and manganese, and also contains some calcium, iron, phosphorus and protein. It's a complex carbohydrate and a good source of dietary fiber.

cooking

• To make **soft polenta**, measure out 2 cups. In a large saucepan, bring 2 quarts of water and 1 t salt to a boil. Lower the heat to a simmer and slowly pour in the polenta, stirring with a whisk until it is blended. When it starts to bubble, reduce heat to the absolute lowest and cook, stirring from time to time, with a wooden spoon, to prevent a skin from forming. It is ready when it falls away from the sides of the saucepan and is very dense and thick. Stir in olive oil (or butter), Parmesan and salt and pepper to taste. Serves 6–8.

• To **grill**, make the polenta as above, but omit the olive oil and Parmesan. When cooked, transfer to an oiled, large flat baking tray. Spread out to form a cake about 1 inch thick. Allow to cool completely and cut into wedges. Brush with olive oil and grill for 3 minutes on each side, until golden.

short order

• Top **grilled polenta wedges** with things like garlicky roasted cherry tomatoes and Parmesan shavings; Parma ham, ricotta and preserved figs; sautéed mixed mushrooms and goat or feta cheese; olive tapenade and marinated artichokes. Serve as a cold snack.

• Serve in place of mashed potatoes to soak up the juices of **rich stews**.

• Serve in place of pasta with a robust **tomato-based sauce**.

• When making polenta, stir in spring onions and lime juice at the end of cooking. Cool; cut into strips (like **French fries**) and grill, turning to brown on all sides. Serve as a snack with sweet chili sauce, or as "chips" with a main meal.

• Use dry in place of **breadcrumbs** to coat fish or chicken. Season uncooked polenta with salt and milled black pepper, add a few finely chopped fresh herbs or grated Parmesan cheese. Dust fish or chicken with flour, dip in egg white and roll in polenta crumbs, patting where there are gaps. Spray with olive oil cooking spray and bake in a preheated 400°F oven, until done.

• Serve large wedges of grilled polenta topped with roasted vegetables and Parmesan shavings. Makes a great **vegetarian meal**.

the dinner party thing

There's no need for you to ever be intimidated again.

I've planned the menus, given you the recipes, and all you have to do is follow the instructions. How easy is that? Here are two beyond-fabulous main-course dishes, and for each there are a few suggestions of what to serve before and/or after. It is totally acceptable to serve two courses instead of three. If you skip dessert, coffee and biscotti or something small, decadent and "chocolatey" will do just fine. I've allowed a little more fat than usual, because dinner parties are special, but where you see an * next to a dish it is almost, if not quite, fat-free.

checklist
- Make sure you have enough ice and glasses, and chill the drinks where necessary.
- Buy fresh flowers — don't forget to put a few in the bathroom.
- Go big on candles — they set the scene and cover a multitude of sins.
- Prepare as much as possible ahead of time. You can even set the table the night before.
- Relax, look beautiful and have fun.

dinner 1
salmon trout on warm lentil salad

Salmon trout (rainbow trout) is substantially lower in fat than ordinary salmon, but this recipe will work perfectly with either.

lentils
2 C brown or green lentils
1½ quarts weak chicken or vegetable stock
1 bay leaf
½ C olive oil
1 t grainy mustard
1 T white wine vinegar
1 bunch green onions, finely chopped
a handful Italian parsley, roughly chopped
olive oil

salmon trout
juice of 1 lemon or lime
8 salmon trout fillets
sea salt and milled black pepper
crème fraîche (optional)
Serves 8

Boil lentils in stock with a bay leaf, until cooked. Meanwhile, mix together olive oil, mustard and vinegar. Drain lentils, pour over olive oil mixture and cover to keep warm. Just before serving, stir in chopped green onion and Italian parsley.

Preheat oven to 400°F. Drizzle fish with lemon/lime juice, and season. Bake for 8–10 minutes. Spoon the lentil mixture onto each plate, top with fish and add a dollop of crème fraîche. Serve with a mixed-leaf salad.

131

Match up with ...

fresh tagliolini with breadcrumbs, chili and garlic

Process half a loaf of stale, white bread in a blender to make a batch of breadcrumbs. Heat a quantity of olive oil in a pan and fry 3 cloves crushed garlic and 2 t dried chili flakes for 2 minutes. Add crumbs and sauté until golden and crisp. Toss through fresh, not dried, egg tagliolini pasta, and serve with extra olive oil and grated Parmesan.

warm tomatoes on bruschetta with arugula pesto

Brush thick slices of Italian bread with a little olive oil on both sides. Place under a preheated grill and toast on one side until golden. Thickly slice 1 ripe tomato and place on untoasted side of bread. Place in the oven, on the second shelf down, and grill to soften the tomato. Arrange on a plate and drizzle with arugula or basil pesto, thinned with a little olive oil.

warm oat cookies with creamed Gorgonzola

Mix together fat-free cream cheese and full-cream Gorgonzola to taste (this is a great way of getting the flavor of Gorgonzola while cutting the fearsome fat content). Pile into a bowl and refrigerate until needed. Warm oatmeal cookies in the oven for a few minutes — not strictly necessary but rather yummy. Top with cheese and serve with fresh grapes and fruit preserves. You will need about ½ pound cream cheese and 5–6 ounces Gorgonzola for 8 people.

ricotta brûlée with peach wedges

Preheat oven to 300°F. Whisk 2 pounds ricotta, 7 ounces confectioners' sugar, 3 eggs and ½ t vanilla extract until smooth. Spoon mixture into 8 greased ramekins or one 8-inch ovenproof bowl. Place ramekins or bowl in a roasting pan with enough boiling water to reach halfway up the dish. Bake for 30 minutes or until just set. Remove and allow to cool for 15 minutes. When ready to serve, melt 1 C brown sugar very slowly in a saucepan. Pour over set ricotta and cool to form a hard crust. Serve with wedges of fresh peaches or apricots.

dinner 2
lemon chicken on herbed orzo

The herbed orzo was inspired by the clever folks at *Australian Gourmet Traveller* magazine.

lemon chicken
½ C olive oil
½ C lemon juice
thinly sliced peel of 2 large lemons
8 large chicken breasts, with skin, bones removed*
sea salt and milled black pepper
½ C chicken stock
Serves 8

Mix olive oil, lemon juice and peel in a bowl; add chicken pieces, coat well and marinate for at least an hour in the fridge. Preheat oven to 425°F. Heat a non-stick frying pan over high heat, season chicken well and place skin-down in pan. Sear until golden on one side, and turn to seal on other side, for 1 minute. Transfer to an ovenproof dish and pour over marinating juices. Add stock and cook for 10–15 minutes until firm and juices run clear. Slice and serve on top of herbed orzo and spoon over sauce.
*Use a very sharp knife to remove the bones from beneath the chicken breast, or ask the butcher to do it for you.

herbed orzo
2 C orzo (pasta rice)
¼ C olive oil
1⅓ pounds spinach, trimmed and washed
handful (½ packet) dill, chopped
4 green onions, chopped finely
1 romaine lettuce, trimmed and shredded
2 handfuls Italian parsley, roughly chopped
handful (½ packet) basil leaves, torn
juice of 1 lemon
Serves 8

Cook pasta in a big pot of salted water, until al dente. Drain, rinse under cold water, drain again and transfer pasta to a large bowl. Add ¼ C olive oil and toss to coat. Pour boiling water over spinach, drain and chop. Add with green onion, lettuce, herbs and lemon to pasta. Season and mix well.

Match up with ...

roasted tomato, red pepper and chili soup

Drizzle 3 halved, seeded red peppers and 3 red chilies with olive oil and roast in a preheated 400°F oven for 20 minutes. Add 10 large, ripe tomatoes, halved, and roast for 15 minutes. Remove and peel peppers and tomatoes. Fry 1 onion and 3 cloves crushed garlic in olive oil in a large pot. Add peppers, chili, tomatoes, 1½ quarts chicken or vegetable stock, 1 t sugar, sea salt and milled black pepper. Cook for 20 minutes. Purée until smooth. Add a handful of torn basil and stir to combine.

salmon tartare with creamed horseradish

Mix 1 pound smoked salmon with 2 T creamed horseradish, 1 T reduced-fat cream and 3 finely chopped green onions. Season to taste and serve with Melba toast.

Campari poached peaches/nectarines

Place 3 C sifted superfine sugar, 5 C water, 1½ C Campari, 1 T grenadine and 1 T lemon juice in a saucepan and bring to a boil. Reduce heat and simmer for 30 minutes. Add 8 peaches or nectarines, cover and simmer for 10–15 minutes or until soft. Remove fruit with a slotted spoon. Pour syrup over nectarines and serve with frozen yogurt.

box of delights

Buy an assortment of good quality nougat, Turkish Delight and chocolate-covered Brazil nuts or chocolate salami (available from good delis). Arrange in little boxes — recycled Camembert cheese boxes, or cardboard boxes from a stationery store, will work a treat.

vegetable basics

Veggies are — or should be — the mainstay of every meal. Here are 34 ideas to keep yourself interested.

foil-baked tomatoes and peppers

foil baking

If you begin to take this side dish thing seriously, foil baking is the logical step. All the goodness of the vegetables is trapped inside a wrapping of foil. (Baking paper works just as well.) Lay the foil flat, fill the center with veggies; fold the foil cleverly, or admit defeat and staple the sides together. Here are a few combos:

• Quarter tomatoes, add chunks of red and yellow pepper, crushed garlic, a handful basil or Italian parsley, olive oil and a glug of white wine. Season, seal and bake in a preheated 400°F oven for about 30 minutes (pictured left).

• Halve baby carrots and zucchini, add a dash of wine and olive oil, a sprig of thyme and a bit of crushed garlic. Season, seal and bake in a preheated 400°F oven for about 30 minutes.

• Combine baby corn, baby carrots, sliced green onions and pattypan squash. Add white wine, olive oil, a pinch of sugar, a few fresh herbs. Seal and bake in a preheated 400°F oven for 30-40 minutes.

spinach

The beads of water that collect on spinach leaves from washing are all the water you need for cooking. Place spinach in a large pot, cover and cook over a medium heat. Or you can get fancy:

• Stir-fry onions and garlic in olive oil. Add a handful of pecan or pine nuts and sauté to brown. Add washed, chopped spinach and cook until wilted. Season and serve.

• Sauté minced chili and garlic in olive oil with a spoon or two of tomato purée. Season with sea salt, pepper and a pinch of sugar. Add washed, chopped spinach and stir-fry until wilted.

• Cook spinach, drain and coarsely chop, and serve at room temperature drizzled with good olive oil and freshly grated Parmesan.

tomatoes

• Halve large ripe tomatoes, scoop out the seeds and discard. Liberally drizzle with olive oil and balsamic vinegar, season with salt, pepper and crushed garlic, and

carrots sauteéd with spices and orange peel

bake in a 350°F oven until soft. Serve as a simple side dish or with bruschetta as part of a starter.

• Roast baby tomatoes in a 350°F oven for 15–20 minutes. When soft and squishy, remove and season liberally with garlic, olive oil, balsamic vinegar, salt and pepper. Toss into salads or serve as an edible garnish with roasts or grilled chicken.

• Heat a spoon or two of sweet chili sauce in a pan. When bubbling, add a few handfuls of baby tomatoes, cook over a medium heat until soft and beginning to burst. Toss in a handful of fresh basil or arugula and serve.

sautéed zucchini and rosa tomatoes

Add a few handfuls of cooked peas and toss to coat. Season well and serve.

eggplant

• Slice thinly, sprinkle with olive oil and sea salt and roast at 400ºF until crispy — like chips.

• Cut into chunks and marinate with chopped red and yellow peppers in olive oil, garlic, a dash of Tabasco and Italian parsley. Roast in a baking tray until almost soft, add halved baby tomatoes and roast for a further couple of minutes. Serve with grated Parmesan and bread, or add them to a salad.

• Grill thinnish slices and wrap them around anything you like, such as mozzarella or cucumber sticks or strips of chicken.

• Throw chunks into your favorite fresh tomato sauce, cook until really soft and gooey, pile onto pasta, pizza or sandwiches and sprinkle with basil.

• Cut thick wedges, brush with olive oil, roll them in spices and roast, with a little water, until soft.

zucchini

• Heat 2 T of sweet chili sauce in a pan, add a dash of olive oil and gently sauté zucchini until sticky and browned. Add a handful of baby tomatoes and cook for about 3–5 minutes. Toss in a bit of fresh coriander and serve (pictured left).

• Sauté onion and garlic in a large pan. Add thick slices of zucchini and cook until beginning to soften. Add a handful of spinach, a dash of white wine, sugar and seasoning. Cook until spinach has wilted and zucchini are soft.

• Steam or sauté chunks of zucchini. When cooked and slightly cooled, toss with chunks of feta cheese, fresh mint and olive oil. Season well and serve at room temperature.

• Pan-fry zucchini in olive oil and garlic. When cooked, toss with freshly grated Parmesan and milled black pepper and serve.

green beans

• Cook beans in a little rapidly boiling water until just done. Toss in a pan with olive oil, garlic and butter beans, and cook to heat through. Serve with Parmesan.

• Sauté cooked green beans with very finely sliced lemon peel and toasted cashew nuts. Season well.

• Slowly stir-fry onion and garlic in olive oil until browned and crisp. Toss in cooked green beans to coat.

peas

• Braise frozen peas in chicken or vegetable stock with wedges of iceberg lettuce. Season with salt and milled pepper and serve. Chunks of soft, boiled potato work well added to this side dish.

• Fry finely chopped onion and lean bacon until crisp.

potatoes

• Roast new potatoes with olive oil, coarse salt and rosemary until crisp on the outside and soft and floury inside. Other good things to add to mashed potatoes are minced garlic; grainy mustard; Parmesan cheese; slow-cooked, crispy, chopped onions; and chopped fresh herbs.

• Roast new potatoes with olive oil until half cooked, spoon over liberal quantities of onion marmalade (see page 80) and roast until sticky and delicious. Or change it up and toss the fully cooked roasted potatoes with a chunky pesto.

• Cook large or new potatoes with their skins, until soft, drain and coarsely mash with grated lemon peel, olive oil and a little crushed garlic.

mushrooms

• Heat yellow mustard seeds in olive oil until they pop. Add sliced mushrooms of your choice, sauté for a minute or two and add a dash of sweet sherry. Season well, cook until soft and serve.

• Sprinkle large black mushrooms with garlic, herbs, soy sauce, lemon juice and olive oil. Season with milled pepper, cover with foil and bake in a preheated 350°F oven for about 30 minutes. Serve with the cooking liquid.

onions and leeks

• Remove the outer layers of skin from baby onions or shallots, halve lengthwise and drizzle with olive oil. Add fresh herbs and roast in a preheated 350°F oven until soft and browned, about 1 hour. Serve with roasts or cold meats and breads.

• Slowly sauté sliced onions and garlic in balsamic vinegar, sugar and olive oil until dark brown and sticky. Season and serve as a relish or topping for meat or chicken.

• Wash leeks well. Place in a pan of simmering chicken or vegetable stock, add a dash of white wine, a sprig of thyme and cook over a medium heat until soft. Serve as is or with grated Parmesan.

root veggies

• Boil parsnips and carrots and mash together with sea salt, black pepper and olive oil or, gasp, butter!

• Boil beets for about 30 minutes. Remove, rinse in cold water and peel. Cut beets into wedges and place in a roasting pan with wedges of red onion and a few whole cloves of garlic. Drizzle with olive oil, add a couple of dried chilies and cover with foil. Bake in a preheated 400°F oven for 30 minutes. Remove foil, drizzle with balsamic vinegar and cook for a further 20–30 minutes, or until soft.

• Sauté sliced, cooked fresh beets in olive oil and garlic. When cooked, stir in liberal quantities of chopped fresh basil, Italian parsley or mint.

potato mashed with pesto and olive oil

conversions

t = teaspoon
T = tablespoon
C = cup
pinch/dash = ⅙₆ t
½ t = 30 drops
1 t = ⅓ T
1 T = 3 t; ½ ounce
¼ C = 4 T; 2 ounces
⅓ C = 5 T + 1 t
½ C = 8 T; 4 ounces
1 C = 16 T

Index